BROADMAN PRESS
Nashville, Tennessee

©Copyright 1989 • Broadman Press
All rights reserved
4250-67

ISBN-0-8054-5067-X
Dewey Decimal Classification: 223.2
Subject Heading: BIBLE. O.T. PSALMS
Library of Congress Catalog Number: 89-816

Printed in the United States of America

Unless otherwise stated, all Scripture quotations are from the King James Version of the Bible.

Scripture quotations marked RSV are from the Revised Standard Version of the Bible, copyrighted 1946, 1952, © 1971, 1973.

Scripture quotations marked GNB are from the *Good News Bible*, the Bible in Today's English Version. Old Testament: Copyright © American Bible Society 1976; New Testament: Copyright © American Bible Society 1966, 1971, 1976. Used by permission.

Scripture quotations marked NASB are from the *New American Standard Bible.* Copyright © The Lockman Foundation, 1960, 1962, 1963, 1968, 1971, 1972, 1973, 1975, 1977. Used by permission.

Scripture quotations marked TLB are from *The Living Bible.* Copyright © Tyndale House Publishers, Wheaton, Illinois, 1971. Used by permission.

Library of Congress Cataloging-in-Publication Data

Powell, Paul W.
  A faith that sings / Paul W. Powell.
    p. cm.
  ISBN 0-8054-5067-X : $6.95
  1. Bible. O.T. Psalms—Sermons. 2. Baptists—Sermons.
3. Southern Baptist Convention—Sermons. 4. Sermons, American.
5. Christian life—Biblical teaching. I. Title.
BS1430.4.P68 1989
223'.206—dc19   89-816
                                                                                            CIP

*To my grandson Jordan Michael,
the joy of my old age*

Contents

Introduction		7
1.	The Road to Genuine Happiness (Psalm 1)	9
2.	Look Down, Then Up (Psalm 8)	18
3.	The Foolishness of Atheism (Psalm 14)	30
4.	The Contemporary Book (Psalm 19)	39
5.	"He's All I Want" (Psalm 23)	51
6.	"Oh, What a Relief It Is!" (Psalm 32)	62
7.	Lessons of Life and Death (Psalm 39)	69
8.	Finding Forgiveness (Psalm 51)	77
9.	Stand Up to Life (Psalm 55)	88
10.	Inner Space (Psalm 66)	98
11.	The Best Argument for Christianity (Psalm 69:6)	109
12.	The Contagion of Enthusiasm (Psalm 69:9)	118
13.	Faith Amid the Fire (Psalm 73)	129
14.	Banishing Discouragement (Psalm 77)	141
15.	The Days Dwindle Down (Psalm 90)	150
16.	Does the Lord Live Here? (Psalm 101:2)	159
17.	We Are Beneficiaries (Psalm 103)	168
18.	Right Now (Psalm 118)	178
19.	Making Peace with Others (Psalm 133)	187
20.	Heavenly Living on Earth (Psalm 139)	197

Introduction

A Texas millionaire allegedly made a strange request in his will. He wanted to be buried in his pink Cadillac. Lots were purchased, and arrangements were made; a huge crane was bought into the cemetery. Then all of his friends encircled the enormous hole in the ground. As the Cadillac-coffin was lowered into the ground, one man exclaimed, "Man, that's really living!"

One of our big problems today is confusing life with death. Evidences of this confusion can be seen everywhere in our society. There are more alcoholics in America than any other country in the world—between twelve and fifteen million. Every twenty-seven seconds, a couple obtains a divorce, pushing the total to one million cases a year. Close to half of all marriages today are expected to end in divorce.

This year some 28,000 Americans will take their own lives; 4,750 of those will be of school age. Those figures are only the tip of the iceberg. They could be 50 percent higher, and ten times as many try and fail. Our murder rate is high, yet more people kill themselves than kill others.

Why? Why so many unhappy people in perhaps the most affluent society that has ever existed? It is not because people despair of life; it is rather that they despair of death. By and large, we know how to make a good living, but we don't know how to make a good life. We can get where we are going faster than our forefathers, but we have nothing to do when we get there. We have learned to save time, but we don't know what to do with the time we save. We have gained more knowledge than any other generation, but, in our eagerness to learn, we have missed truth itself. We have everything to live with and nothing to live for.

We must get back to the basics—the nuts and bolts of life. That is what this book is about. The wisdom of God found in the Psalms presents timeless truths about living life at its best. It begins by emphasizing the importance of being rightly related to God, the Source of life, and showing how we may live in constant fellowship with Him. Then it emphasizes the importance of good relationships with others—our friends, our family, and our neighbors. Lastly, it shows the importance of our own self-image. When these three relationships are right, life is at its best.

If you are sick and tired of being sick and tired, this book is for you! It was written to help you find the life God wants you to have—so you can have a faith that sings with the psalmist.

1
The Road to Genuine Happiness
(Psalm 1)

Several years ago while I was on a trip to the Amazon Valley of Brazil, missionary Lonnie Doyle told me of the last major anti-evangelical persecution that occurred in the city of Manaus. An angry mob attacked a church and virtually destroyed everything but the four walls. They tore the Bibles and hymnals into pieces and scattered the congregation into the night. Lonnie barely escaped with his life. For six months thereafter the government posted troops around the church to protect the worshipers from the hooligans.

About a year later a man came to Edward Lessa, pastor of the church, to confess that he was the one who had led the mob that fateful night. The man told Pastor Lessa that at the time he had thought he was doing right and that he was proud when he made the Protestants flee. But the next day on his way to the marketplace he found a single page out of one of the Bibles he had helped destroy. The page contained Psalm 1. He told the pastor that he read and reread the first Psalm until he came under conviction. Then he said, "I have since become a believer in Jesus Christ, and I have come to ask you and the church to forgive me for the wrong I did."

That Brazilian man was neither the first nor the last person to be blessed by Psalm 1. It has been a source of inspiration and guidance since it was written centuries ago. One reason it has been so influential is that it gives us such a clear description of a righteous man—his character and his blessings.

David's description begins.

> Blessed is the man that walketh not in the counsel of the ungodly, nor standeth in the way of sinners, nor sitteth in the seat of the scornful. But his delight is in the law of the Lord; and in his law doth he meditate day and night (vv. 1-2).

The Scriptures are clear: the righteous person is one who does not associate with evil men in such a way as to become digressively one of them. We, of course, must associate with all sorts of people if we are going to reach them for Christ. But we must be careful, for sin has a subtle, almost irresistible appeal that draws its victims into a deeper and deeper involvement.

Anyone who considers himself strong enough to control sin should heed the warning of these two verses. Both the nouns and verbs show the progressive nature of sin. Look first at the three verbs of verse 1. The word "walk" suggests a casual acquaintance with sinful men. The word "stand" suggests a closer association with them. And the word "sit" suggests complete absorption into their activities.

Now look at the nouns. They show the same kind of downward pull in the seriousness of sin. The word "ungodly" describes a man who is occasionally out of step with right conduct. The word "sinners" describes those whose wicked conduct becomes habitual. The word "scornful" describes one who has become so hardened and arrogant that he mocks God.

If we are not careful, we may begin in casual fellowship,

walking with those who are occasionally out of step with right living. But once we allow sin to begin, it can drag us along in the undertow until we become so absorbed in its activities that we sit in the "seat of the scornful," hardened, and at ease in sin.

How can we avoid this? There is only one way. We must live continuously in the Word of God (v. 2). We must delight in His law, the whole revelation of the Lord, and meditate in it both day and night. The word "delight" means to derive pleasure from it. God's Word literally lights up the life of the godly person, and he meditates on God's word day and night.

To meditate means simply to direct your thoughts on a subject for a period of time. The Lord commanded Joshua,

> This book of the law shall not depart out of thy mouth; but thou shalt meditate therein day and night, that thou mayest observe to do according to all that is written therein: for then thou shalt make thy way prosperous, and then thou shalt have good success (Josh. 1:8).

This may seem crude, but it certainly makes a point: meditation has been compared to a cow chewing her cud. Cows chew their food two separate times to digest it. They chew it once, swallow it, then bring it up again, and chew it the second time. The once-swallowed food is called a cud. In the same process, so we must keep bringing God's Word into our minds again and again and reflecting upon it. We dare not become so busy with incidentals that we do not have time to meditate on the Word of God.

So David declared that a righteous person is the one who does not associate with sinners in such a way as to become "one of them." Instead, he both delights in and meditates on God's word continuously.

David told us three characteristics of such a righteous man's life: he is happy, he is fruitful, and he is eternal—he will live forever.

Happiness and Holiness

David's description of a righteous man begins with the word "Blessed," which means "joyously happy." This is the chief characteristic of a righteous man; he is incredibly joyous.

Happiness is the supreme quest of most people today, but they are seeking it in the wrong places. They seek it in material possessions—big cars, big houses, and big bucks; they seek it in alcohol and drugs; they seek it in a new mistress or a new mate; and they seek it in vacation trips to exotic places. But they search in vain. Happiness is found in none of those places and in none of those things.

The fact is, happiness is not found in seeking it at all. Happiness is a by-product of righteousness.

There is a story of a dog who commented to his canine friend one day, "I've discovered that happiness is in my tail. So I spend my days chasing my tail, day in and day out, day in and day out." His friend replied, "I discovered the same thing years ago, but I also discovered that, if I'll go on my way, my tail will follow right behind."

Happiness is like that. You do not find it by chasing it. You find it by going through life in righteous living, and it follows after you. Happiness then is the by-product of a godly life.

Jesus began the Sermon on the Mount with the phrase, "Blessed are the . . ." (Matt. 5). After each of the nine uses of that phrase, He listed one of the qualities of life that makes for happiness. These are the same qualities that make for righteousness.

The best-kept secret in life is this: holiness and happiness are inseparably bound together. So, if you would have real joy, the fullness of joy, an abiding joy which nothing can take away, be holy as God is holy. Holiness is blessedness.

Life with A Purpose

The second characteristic of a righteous person is fruitfulness. Early in my Christian experience I learned that there were three "Fs" in the Christian life. They were *facts, faith,* and *feelings.* And they come in that sequence. The Christian life is founded in facts—the fact of sin, the fact that we cannot save ourselves by being religious or by being good, and the fact that Jesus Christ is the one and only Savior.

Next, we respond to those facts by putting our faith and trust in Him. Then and only then do the feelings come. Some people delay becoming a Christian because they are waiting for a "special feeling," but it never comes because it is not supposed to. The feeling does not come until we respond to the facts in faith.

It was years later that I learned about a fourth "F" in the Christian life—fruit. Over fifty times the New Testament declares that a Christian is to bring forth fruit. Whenever anything is mentioned that often in the Word of God, we had better pay attention to it. Paul wrote to the church in Rome that he had often wanted to visit them so he "might have some fruit from among them" (Rom. 1:13). And Jesus made it plain, "Herein is my Father glorified, that you bear much fruit" (John 15:8).

What is the secret of fruitfulness in life? Jesus said, "He that abideth in me, and I in him, the same bringeth forth much fruit" (John 15:5). David declared here that it results from having our lives rooted deeply in the truth of God's Word. The two are essentially the same.

Notice how he described the righteous man, "And he shall be like a tree planted by the rivers of water, that bringeth forth his fruit in his season; his leaf also shall not wither; and whatsoever he doeth shall prosper" (v. 3).

The word "planted" literally means "transplanted." It suggests the idea of planning. This tree is not where it is by accident or by chance but by the will of the gardener. He has carefully transplanted it by the water where it can be nourished and become productive.

We are not here by chance or by accident. God has put us here for a purpose. We are here to be productive and fruitful for God. Only as we live in righteousness can this happen. As we live right and go deeper into God's Word, the fruit grows naturally.

Ronald Prince, a pastor friend, told me his father taught him that he should continually ask himself, "Am I now engaged in the thing for which I came into life?" That is one of life's most important questions. Are you? Only the fruitful person can say, "Yes."

What is the fruit of a godly life? Paul told us that "the fruit of the Spirit is love, joy, peace, longsuffering, gentleness, goodness, faith, Meekness, temperance" (Gal. 5:22-23). He is actually painting for us the perfect picture of Jesus in this cluster of fruit. So, when the New Testament speaks of fruit, it refers to becoming like Christ.

Adoniram Judson was once asked by reporters if it were true that people were comparing him to the apostle Paul. He replied, "If that be true, I am sorry that it is being said: I don't want to be like Paul; I want to be like Jesus." The goal of the Christian life is never to become like Paul or

Peter or any other New Testament character but to become like Jesus Christ Himself!

Fruit in the Christian life, then, is the life of Jesus produced in the life of the believer through the Holy Spirit; and the fruit of the Christian life is the life of Jesus reproduced through the life of the believer in somebody else.

People who live without God eventually live barren and withered lives. Lord Byron wrote:

> My days are in the yellow leaf;
> The flowers and fruits of love are gone;
> The worm, the canker, and the grief
> Are mine alone!

Apart from the righteousness of the word of God, our lives have no roots, no depth, no permanence, and we have no lasting joy. We too soon come to the "yellow leaf" of life.

The Righteous Shall Stand

The final characteristic of a righteous man is permanence. He has eternal life. He will live forever. Note the stark contrast between the righteous and the ungodly.

> [The righteous are] like a tree planted by the rivers of water.... The ungodly are not so: but are like the chaff which the wind driveth away. Therefore the ungodly shall not stand in the judgment, nor sinners in the congregation of the righteous. For the Lord knoweth the way of the righteous: but the way of the ungodly shall perish (vv. 3-6).

That word "perish" is frightening. It literally means "to be lost." The manner of life of all people, the righteous as well as the ungodly, is carefully observed by God. He knows our ways. The ungodly cannot stand, they cannot abide before Him in the judgment. They will ultimately be lost—lost to joy, lost to peace, lost from God, lost for eternity.

Most people cannot endure the thought of that for themselves or for their loved ones. God has placed eternity in our hearts. We long for immortality. We cannot bear the thought that life ends at the cemetery, of never seeing our loved ones again. And we need not. For God's people shall live and abide forever.

Recently I read a story from Irish history that set me to thinking. Times were hard and thousands of persons were unemployed. To counter the high unemployment, the Irish government embarked on an ambitious road-building project. Many new jobs were created. Workers enthusiastically joined the project. Happy to be engaged in a significant task that would both feed their families and benefit their society, the workers sang as they worked.

But after awhile, the workers' level of motivation underwent a dramatic downturn. The work slowed and the singing ceased. Why? The workers discovered the roads led nowhere. The road-building project had been concocted only to provide jobs.

People without God are like those workers. They are on a road to nowhere. They are living a life in which there is no future.

We can be happy, our lives can be fruitful and meaningful, and we can live forever with Christ. The secret in Psalm 1 is to plant our lives in God's righteousness and grow in Him.

This kind of life is available to all of us in Jesus Christ. Paul wrote to the Roman church, "Christ is the end of the law for righteousness to everyone that believeth" (Rom. 10:4). Then he added,

> That if thou shalt confess with thy mouth the Lord Jesus,

and shalt believe in thine heart that God hath raised him from the dead, thou shalt be saved. For with the heart man believeth unto righteousness; and with the mouth confession is made unto salvation (vv. 9-10).

A man had just purchased an old Model-T Ford. As he drove the old car home, though, it stopped on a lonely stretch of highway. The stranded motorist had not the slightest idea what was wrong. Presently, an apparently wealthy man in a gleaming new Lincoln pulled up beside him and asked if he could help. "Anything you can do will be appreciated," replied the owner of the ancient Ford. The stranger uncovered the engine compartment, quickly made an adjustment on the old carburetor, and set the spark lever on the steering column exactly right. Then, as he turned the crank, the old "Tin Lizzie" started running like new.

The amazed and grateful owner gushed, "Thank you, Sir. You've helped me, and I don't even know your name."

"You're quite welcome," he answered. "My name is Henry Ford." You see, Henry Ford knew how to make the Model T run because he had made it to begin with. The same is true with God and our lives. God can make us run smoothly because He made us in the first place!

2
Look Down, Then Up
(Psalm 8)

One night several years ago a drifter took his own life in New York City's Central Park. The only identification the police could find on his person was a crudely scribbled note that read, "I'm a nothing, an absolute nobody. I'm just a peanut in Yankee Stadium. I've decided to step on myself once and for all."

Those words illustrate quite graphically the relationship between what one thinks about oneself and what one does to oneself. They emphasize the importance of a person's self-image.

The starting point for both success and happiness is a healthy self-image. It is the core of one's personality. It affects every aspect of human behavior: the ability to learn, the capacity to grow and change, the choice of friends, a mate, and a career.

Since this is true, learning who we are and liking who we are is essential to having an abundant life. That is why Psalm 8 is so important. It helps us like no other passage in the Bible to get acquainted with ourselves. It asks and answers the question of the ages, "What is man?"

This haunting question has been asked by theologians, philosophers, and thinkers since the beginning of time. The answer we come up with depends on whom we ask. If you could ask scientist Charles Darwin, "What is man?"

he might answer, "Man is the climax of the evolutionary process—a monkey's uncle." Ask Communist Karl Marx, "What is man?" and he would likely answer, "Man is an economic tool—a producing animal." Ask psychologist Sigmund Freud, "What is man?" and he would probably answer, "Man is a bundle of sexual drives—a mating primate."

But we know that man is more than a monkey, a materialist, or a sex maniac. These are all inadequate views. If you want to know the true identity of man, you must ask God. He gives us His answer here.

The psalmist began and ended his meditation with an expression of praise to God: "O Lord our Lord, how excellent [i.e. majestic, magnificent] is thy name in all the earth!" (vv. 1, 9).

Wherever the psalmist looked, he beheld the magnificence of God. He saw His glory in both the highest star and in the smallest child. He saw His majesty in both physical nature and in human nature—man. But he saw man as the highest expression of God's glory in the universe.

The psalmist's inquiry probably began one night when he gazed into the heavens and viewed the moon and the stars, the handiwork of God. As he thought about the vastness of space and the smallness of human beings, the immensity of the heavens and human frailty, he was awed to humility. He asked himself, "What is man that God should pay so much attention to him? Why are we so special to God? Why does He care so much for us?"

It is significant that David's contemplation of humanity began with God. He did not make the popular mistake of starting with mankind in his effort to understand mankind. The thinker who starts with persons has nowhere else to go. The one who starts with God has the opportunity to see how we are related to Him and how all things fit into a divine pattern—all things including mankind!

David addressed God as "Lord" or "Yahweh," the sovereign ruler of the universe. The Lord was his Master. He felt in awe of the One whose hand controlled all things. Once we know who God is, then we can begin to understand who we are. Until we start with God we start at no beginning, and we work to no end.

With his naked eye David probably could see only five or six thousand stars. Today with the use of the telescope, we realize there are one hundred billion stars in our galaxy alone. And there are at least ten billion galaxies the size of ours in the known universe! If you were to try to cross our galaxy, traveling at the speed of light—186,000 miles per second—it would take eighty thousand years to go from one end to the other. If you wanted to travel to the farthest object we can see in the universe, it would require ten million years to arrive there.

If David were awed to humility by the immensity of space and the seeming frailty of man, how much more we ought to be.

When we consider all of creation, humanity is but a speck of cosmic dust—but we are a special speck—a thinking speck made in the image of God. We are the object of God's loving care.

There are three great truths concerning mankind in this psalm. Understanding them is essential to knowing who we are and to living life with dignity.

According to David, humanity is the object of God's affection; the crown of God's creation; and the custodian of God's world.

Somebody Up There Loves You

One thing is apparent in Scripture. God likes mankind. He was pleased with what He made.

At a gala banquet to honor poet Carl Sandburg's seventy-fifth birthday, photographer Edward Steichen said, "On the day that God made Carl, He didn't do anything else in that day but sit around and feel good" (quoted by Val Lauder in *The New York Times*). That's what God did when He made Adam. He looked at the man whom He had created and exclaimed, "That is good. That is very good!" And we can believe with assurance that He did the same the day He made us. As God liked Adam and Carl, so He likes you and me.

David spoke about the special place we have in the heart of God when he asked, "What is man, that thou art mindful of him? and the son of man, that thou visiteth him?" (v. 4). The word *mindful* means "to mark out." The word *visiteth* means "to care for." God has marked mankind out as the special object of His love and care. He loves us and delights in us as He delights in no other part of His workmanship.

I hope you will never forget how much God loves you, and as a result I hope you will also love yourself. While you and I must frankly face our sinfulness, we must go on without hating ourselves. We must not hate what God loves so very much.

Years ago Isaac Watts wrote a hymn entitled, "Alas, and Did My Savior Bleed." In the original words of that song the writer told of Jesus dying on the cross, "For such a worm as I." In a newer version that line has been changed to "for sinners such as I." Now, when we sing that song I still get mixed up and often I am the only worm in the house! But I'm glad we changed it. Nowhere in all of God's word do we hear Him address us as worms. Sometimes people in the Bible call themselves worms, but God is always saying, "My son, My daughter, I love you."

Even the severest of His judgments and the sharpest of His denunciations in Scripture are aimed at getting us to put ourselves in a position to receive His love.

We are special to God. We are the object of His affection.

Dust and Deity

The second thing David said about man is, "Thou hast made him a little lower than the angels" (v. 5).

For years many of the best brains have contended that mankind is the chance product of circumstances in a universe that is itself the freak result of unknown occurrences, that we are the accidental result of an evolutionary process. This view has been particularly popular among those who find it hard or uncomfortable to believe in God. Through this belief they have been able to free themselves from religious concepts and systems of morality and to produce their own substitutes. Their lifestyle has reflected these substitute standards and in most instances have proved extremely attractive to contemporary society.

Yet, there is one problem, that unbelieving man has been unable to avoid: the dehumanizing effect of this kind of thinking. It is humiliating to believe that man is an accident and of little importance. The theories that lead people to believe that mankind merely "happened" also logically lead them to believe that one's life is meaningless, and that is dehumanizing. However, there is nothing dehumanizing about the psalmist's understanding of man. His great conviction is "Thou hast made him . . ."

In spite of all the harsh attacks against the biblical view

Look Down, Then Up

of man, I must state quite firmly that nowhere else is such a high view of mankind taught. From no other source will man ever gain the impression that he is anything more than a puzzle living in the middle of a muddle. But the Bible insists that man is the intelligent product of an intelligent Creator.

Genesis 1:27 tells us that God formed man out of the dust of the earth and then breathed into him the breath of life, and man became a living soul. He created man in His own image and gave him dominion over all of creation. We are, then, both of dust and of divinity.

The Scriptures not only tell us our origin but also give us our position in creation. "Thou hast made him a little lower than the angels." To be a little lower than the angels is far, far better than being a little higher than the apes!

This is actually a poor translation of the original language. The word translated "angels" is the Hebrew name "Elohim." It is one of the most common names for God in the Bible. Genesis 1:1 says, "In the beginning [Elohim] created the heaven and the earth." So, in reality, mankind was made, not a little lower than the angels, but a little lower than God Himself! We are made in the image of God—next to God.

God wanted fellowship with human beings, so He made us different from the other animals. Human kinship with beast is time's oldest lie. Friend, we are not kin to the animals. We are kin to God. We are made from the dust but kin to God.

What does it mean to be made in the image of God? In what ways are we like Him? We are like God in that we are rational, moral, and spiritual beings. We are like God in that we have intelligence: we can think, we can dream, we can reason, and we can remember.

Animals act on instinct; persons act intelligently. Have

you ever tried to teach geology to an elephant? Astronomy to an eagle? Theology to a dog? It can't be done! But you can teach all three to the most primitive savage from the darkest jungle because he has the light of intelligence in him.

We are like God in that we are thinking, rational beings. The human brain is the most complex mechanism in the world. Some people have compared it to a sophisticated computer, but technology hasn't even come close to duplicating its capabilities. Dr. Gerhard Dirks, who holds fifty inventive ideas from studying the functions of the human brain, commented on its complexity: "If we could invent a computer that would duplicate the capabilities of the human brain, it would take a structure the size of the Empire State Building just to house it."

We are also like God in that we are moral beings. We have a conscience: a sense of right and wrong and the capacity to choose between the two. A bull may gore his owner, a horse may trample his rider, a lion may maul his trainer, and feel no guilt over what it did because it does not know the difference. But we not only know the way things are, we know the way they ought to be. We have a conscience that tells us some things are right and some things are wrong.

People are the only creatures that both laugh and cry, because we are the only ones who know the difference between the way things are and the way things ought to be. We are the only creatures who blush, because we are the only ones capable of being embarrassed by our actions.

We are like God in that we have a spirit. Man is not only the only creature who laughs, weeps, and blushes, he is also the only one who commits suicide, because he is the only one who is capable of being bored with his existence.

This boredom is a sign of humanity's higher heredity. We realize there is more to life than animal existence. We were made for fellowship with God and our life is incomplete without Him. As Augustine put it, "Thou hast made us for thyself, and our hearts are restless till they find rest in thee."

A Child Of the King

"Thou hast crowned him with glory and honor," David sang. This language is commonly used to refer to kings. God has made us the royal princes of His universe. That's who we are.

The dignity and worth of a person does not depend on what he does, where he lives, what he has, or who his ancestors are. It depends on the fact that he is made in the image of God.

My friend Dr. Bob Gehring explained, "I never introduce myself as a doctor. I never relate my identity to my profession—who I am to what I do. If I did, when I quit doing I would quit being. I have an intrinsic value separate from what I do. I am a child of God."

Human injustice and racial prejudices arise when people forget about human dignity as God created us. Every person in the world—regardless of education, racial background, economic, or social status—has been made in God's image and thus has an intrinsic worth.

Nelda Davis sent me a poster yesterday that pictured a little boy saying, "I know I'm somebody 'cause God don't make no junk."

Peter E. Long expressed this same truth in his beautiful poem: "In His Image."

> In a little lighted mission
> Stands a derelict at the door,

> As he comes to be united
> With the Savior we adore.
>
> Shall we weigh him in the balance
> At the money lender's rate
> And consign him to the vermin
> And the vice of his estate?
>
> Shall we banish from our vision
> All the cost he represents
> That our Savior has expended
> For the sinner who repents?
>
> In this derelict in the doorway
> Dwells the image of our Lord
> And the price of his departure
> Is the price we can't afford!

No matter who you are or what you have done, you have been made in the image of God, and you are one of the crowning glories of creation. You are made to be a child of the King, and that makes you somebody. You may be living below your status as a child of the King, but you are a potential child nonetheless.

Made to Rule

The third truth of this psalm is that God has made mankind the custodian, the manager of His universe. Humanity's royal status can be seen in the lordship that is assigned to us. We were made to rule. The Lord gave us dominion over the works of His hand and put all things under our feet. God even names some of them—sheep, oxen, all the beasts of the field and the fowl of the air, the fish of the sea, and everything that passes in the sea. Everything in the earth, everything above the earth, everything in the sea. That's everything there is.

One fact is clear: God made a fantastic world and then

Look Down, Then Up

set mankind loose in it to explore and to develop it. Man was charged with the responsibility to use his God-given talents to discover the resources of the earth and to develop them to their fullest. What a challenge to human creativity and ingenuity! What a remarkable job He has done!

We have explored the wilderness and found coal, oil, iron, and salt. We have spanned rivers, dammed the lakes, built roads, houses, cities, and cars. We have made contact lenses, laser beams, televisions, and satellites in the sky. We have found a cure for tuberculosis and a vaccine for polio. We have transplanted hearts and kidneys, created music, paintings, and sculpture.

Even Darwin acknowledged human superiority when he said, "Man has become, even in his rudest state, the dominant animal that ever appeared on this earth."

Mankind has come a long way from the day when God made him to have dominion. In fact, we subdued everything in the world and then headed for space, looking for other worlds to conquer. But there is one thing we have not been able to subdue—ourselves. God gave us the capacity to control and govern, but we have failed to govern ourselves. Herein lies the root of the human dilemma.

"Man," wrote Pascal, "is both the glory and the scum of the universe." We explore but we also exploit. We educates but we also eradicate. We produce but we also pollute. We made the scalpel but also shrapnel. Human beings invented the gas chambers of Auschwitz; however, other human beings also entered those gas chambers upright with the Twenty-third Psalm or the Lord's Prayer on their lips.

Man is both the golden boy and the black sheep of our world. He is the unquestioned master of all the earth's resources and the undoubted mastermind behind most of the world's ills. Whatever is wrong with the world is certainly not due to the giraffes or the bumblebees. It is due to us.

What is the matter? What went wrong with mankind? God endowed us with the power of choice. He didn't create robots programmed to worship and obey Him. He gave mankind a free will, the ability to choose. And persons, as we know in Genesis 3, deliberately chose to disobey God, to sin. The result: the image of God has been marred, defaced.

Only human beings were given the power to choose. No one ever pats a puppy on the head and asks what he is going to be when he grows up. We are aware he is going to be a dog. But a boy or girl is different. A child can grow up to be any number of things. God gave us choices, and our choices have led to our own downfall.

The answer to the human dilemma comes from the New Testament use of the psalm we are considering. "But we see Jesus, who was made a little lower than the angels for the suffering of death, crowned with glory and honour" (Heb. 2:9, *a*).

The point of this statement is that the Lord of glory, our Lord Jesus, took human form for the expressed purpose of tasting "death for every man" (v. 9*b*). But why was this necessary? In order that through His death he might destroy "him that hath power of death, that is, the devil," and deliver all of us from his bondage (Heb. 2:14-15).

Here is the clue. Man, the great and glorious king of the world, is in bondage to the devil because of sin.

So the picture is clear. Mankind, made in the image of God to rule and reign as the divine agent in charge of the earth, rejected his place and opened himself to the devil. The devil then took brilliant humanity and began to manipulate us to the ultimate destruction of both us and the world. But Jesus came and, through His death and resurrection, dealt the devil a body blow and offered freedom from the devil's dominion to all who will acknowledge Him and reject the devil.

Deliverance from the devil means considerably more than eventual bliss in heaven. It is much more than "pie-in-the-sky-by-and-by." It has to do with people being free from the devil's influence to such a degree that we can become more like the people we were initially created to be—free to subdue the earth for the purposes of God rather than human greed, liberated from devilish dynamics and brought unto the power of divine principle. Now the broken image of God that shines in Jesus Christ (2 Cor. 4:4; Col. 1:15) can be restored in us when we turn to God in repentance and humble faith.

Lest we should be absorbed in the contemplation of our greatness, the psalmist closes as he began—by reminding us of our subordinate rank. Man has dignity, but God alone has majesty. We are in the image of God, but we are not gods. Majesty and dominion are the possession of God. When we turn to Him He can restore our lost glory.

3
The Foolishness of Atheism
(Psalm 14)

In June of 1963, the United States Supreme Court, acting on a case initiated by Madelyn Murray O'Hair, declared that compulsory prayer in the public schools was unconstitutional. That decision catapulted Mrs. O'Hair into the position of "America's foremost atheist." Since that time many people have been appalled at what Mrs. O'Hair thinks about God. Psalm 14 tells us what God thinks about Mrs. O'Hair.

You might think that the Bible is full of verses about atheism. Not so! The atheist is referred to only once in the entirety of Scripture: "The fool hath said in his heart, There is no God" (Ps. 14:1). Nothing more is added. Nothing more is written.

The Bible begins with the tremendous avowal, "In the beginning God created the heaven and the earth" (Gen. 1:1). Having stated the overwhelming and self-evident fact of God, the Scripture thereafter never discusses the possibility of His nonexistence. His reality is never debated or called into question again.

Such a fact is astonishing. It is amazing that the entire Bible should refer to the atheist as a fool and then pass him by with no further notice. However, that is exactly what God does.

The Hebrew word for "fool" is *nadal,* which literally

means "stupid." Why does God call the atheist stupid and then say nothing else about him? It is because the atheist lives like a fool, thinks like a fool, and dies like a fool.

He Lives Like a Fool

The psalmist begins by picturing God as looking down from heaven upon persons. The word *look* is the common Hebrew word for describing a man stooping down to peer out a window or leaning over the railing of a balcony in order to gain a clearer view of the situation below. As God looked down on the earth in Noah's day in disgust, and as He looked down on Sodom and Gomorrah with revulsion, so He looks down on us today. What is He looking for? He is looking to see who acknowledges His existence and seeks after Him.

What God sees as He looks down on us is a morally bankrupt society. People are not seeking after Him. Instead they have all become "corrupt," "abominable," and "filthy." These are ever and always the fruit of atheism. It can produce nothing else.

Atheism can never produce a noble nation or a righteous people. One reason is: without God there is no basis for absolute right and wrong. When people reject God, they destroy the foundation for moral and ethical behavior.

As a flower cut from its roots will soon wither and die, so we are a cut-flower civilization. You cannot have fruits without roots. If we want the fruit of law and order in society, truth and honesty in government, security and stability in the home, we must return to the roots of our faith and trust in God.

A final court of appeals for settling all moral and spiritual questions is necessary to avoid hopeless confusion. If there is no authority in life, one must decide for himself what is right and what is wrong. As finite beings we must act as if we were infinite, and since that is impossible, we are driven to complete insecurity, anxiety, and despair.

Historians have long recognized this fact. No lesser historian than Will Durant affirmed this in his book *The Lessons of History*. This book is a summary of his larger, ten-volume work, *The Story of Civilization,* and represents the cream of his thinking after forty years of studying history. In it he said, concerning religion, ". . . even the skeptical historian develops a humble respect for religion since he sees it function in every land and in every age." Then he relates many of the good things that have come into the world as a result of religion. Finally, he stated this interesting fact about morals: "There is no significant example in history, before our time, of a society successfully maintaining moral life without the aid of religion."

David Klein came to virtually the same conclusion in a *Reader's Digest* article entitled "Is There a Substitute for God?" He pointed out that much of the moral decline in America today is nothing more than a backlash from the fact that we have tried to substitute other things for God and, consequently, our whole moral foundation has crumbled.

Even Sigmund Freud observed, "Ethical rules lose their power in a faithless society." It is as simple as that. If there is no God, all is permissible. People cannot sow a materialistic humanism for six decades without greasing the skids of moral decay, and that is exactly what we have done.

When I look at America today I feel like Billy Sunday did in his day. He quipped, "I used to say that society was going to the dogs, but I've quit saying that out of respect for the dogs." And on another occasion he commented,

"At the rate America is decaying morally, we will soon have to change our national symbol from the eagle to a vulture."

I am not claiming that all who deny God and leave Him out of their lives will end up in the gutter. Sin sometimes takes on a high polish. It is not always beer and the barroom. Sometimes it is champagne and the country club. Sin sometimes even joins the church and sits among the saints on Sunday morning. But, when it does, it is the same old sin. And it it apt to describe it as God describes it here—"corrupt," "abominable," and "filthy."

In spite of what the atheist claims or how he lives, there is a God, and His laws are both universal and eternal. When God spoke to Moses on Mount Sinai, He didn't give ten suggestions. He gave Ten *Commandments*. What God spoke in those commandments are absolutes for all people of all ages. Right is right because God said so, and wrong is wrong because God said so. Moreover, if a thing was wrong yesterday, it is wrong today, and it will be forever and eternally wrong. If a thing was once right, it is still right today, and if the world shall last a million years it will also be right then.

But the atheist has no God and no moral and ethical foundation for his life. The end result is riot and ruin. He lives like a fool.

He Thinks Like a Fool

Atheism is not only morally bankrupt, it is also intellectually bankrupt. The atheist thinks like a fool. Almost as if in disbelief, God asks concerning these atheists, "Have all the workers of iniquity no knowledge?" (v. 4).

The Hebrew word for *knowledge* means "to know by seeing." God is self-evident to those who will look with an open mind.

Immanuel Kant said, "Two things fill the mind with ever-increasing wonder and awe, . . . the starry heavens above me and the moral law within me."

Atheism has no answer for the vast mystery of the universe or the meaning of man's life on earth. No answer whatsoever!

We do have a universe on our hands. It demands an explanation. Where did it come from? We have two choices. Either the universe made itself or Someone made it.

The more we study the universe—its vastness, its complexity, its preciseness—the more convincing proof there is that it could not have made itself. Nor could it have resulted from an accident. Behind a universe that displays so much intelligence, accuracy, beauty, and power, there is bound to be a God of intelligence and power who brought it all into being.

To believe that a universe as vast, complex, and precise as ours could have made itself is sheer stupidity. Do you know of anything else that made itself?

As Professor Edwin Conklin, the distinguished Princeton University biologist, once wrote, "The probability of life originating from an accident is comparable to the probability of the unabridged dictionary resulting from an explosion in a printing factory." I agree.

Nature's witness to God is silent, persistent, and universal. To the person who has a mind to think, eyes to see, ears to hear, it will always speak of God. God is so self-evident and so reasonable that only a sheer fool would deny His existence.

Having raised a question about the lunacy of an unbelieving world, God then gives two examples of the foolish thinking of atheism—its disregard for human life and its prayerlessness.

Atheistic thinking, if allowed to run its course, eventually comes to a total disregard for human life and an unbelievable and incomprehensible cruelty. In the eyes of the atheist, people are expendable. After all, if there is no God, then man is not made in His image and is of no more importance than an animal. He has no intrinsic value. He is expendable. Taken to its extremities atheism becomes cruel, inhuman, and even insane.

This is what happened in Nazi Germany. Reinhold Niebuhr said concerning pre-World War II Germany that it had more education "per square head" than anywhere else in the world. But Nazism rejected God. Its leaders were determined to build a super race. They would be the only God needed. To "purify the race," six million Jews were executed in gas chambers.

Why not? If there is no God, then there is no ultimate morality and mankind has no value. It is but a step from atheism to the gas chamber—in Germany or anywhere else.

Soviet Russia is another example of what I have in mind. In countless classrooms across the world today where Communism prevails, the teacher walks into the classroom and greets the class by saying, "There is no God," and the class responds, "No, and there never has been."

What has this kind of thinking produced? The Siberian slave camps and other unbelievable kinds of inhumanity.

Alexander Solzhenitsyn declared that Stalin, at the height of his power, was executing forty thousand people a month. It is but a step from atheism to the Siberian slave camp and the slaughter of "dissidents."

If there is no God, there is no man in the highest sense of the word. Man becomes nothing more than an animal —a producing animal—expendable, according to the whims of those who are in power.

No atheistic movement has ever founded and maintained an orphanage, a hospital, or a great university. Atheists do not unite to organize to feed the hungry, visit the sick, or care for the poor and needy. No atheist country has ever established and maintained a government of the people, by the people, and for the people.

Atheism also produces a bold and arrogant pride. The atheist does not call upon the Lord in prayer. In his self-sufficiency he feels independent of God.

If a person should remark to me, "I am an atheist; there is no God," I would reply, "Sir, have you been everywhere there is to go? Have you seen everything there is to see? Do you know all there is to know? Have you had every experience there is to have?"

No one has been everywhere, seen everything, had every experience, or possessed total knowledge. So unless he is an absolute and unqualified fool, his answer will be "No!"

I would then suggest to him, "Perhaps, then, God is to be found in one of those places you have never been. Maybe He is to be known in that particle of knowledge you do not yet possess. Maybe God can be seen and felt in one of those experiences you have not yet had."

For someone to state with any certainty "There is no God" is to claim more than any person can possibly know. I can understand how a person could confess "I am an agnostic—I do not know if there is a God." But to assume the position of an atheist is to play the fool. It is one matter to say, "There is no God in my experience." It is an altogether different matter to say, "There is no God in existence." The first is a confession of ignorance. The second is a confession of arrogance.

He Dies Like a Fool

Not only is atheism morally bankrupt and intellectually bankrupt, it is also spiritually bankrupt. The atheist lives like a fool, thinks like a fool, and eventually dies like a fool.

"There were they," writes the psalmist, "in great fear: for God is in the generation of the righteous" (v. 5). This verse is obviously prophetic. It points to the future when all men will stand before God. When that time comes, the atheist will tremble in the presence of the Almighty. Then he will realize that there is a God who has been dwelling among His people all the while.

Death is a part of life. As George Bernard Shaw once observed, "Life's ultimate statistic is the same for all men —one out of one dies." And the Bible declares, "It is appointed unto man once to die, but after this the judgment" (Heb. 9:27).

When we die, we must face God. Atheism offers no comfort in the hour of death and no hope for eternity. Hence, the atheist must die like a fool—in fear and trembling.

Several years ago a prison chaplain told me that the warden of the Walls Unit of the Texas Department of Correction in Huntsville had witnessed the execution of every one of the fifty-six men who had been put to death in the state's electric chair during the history of that unit.

Some of them were hard and calloused men. "But," the warden mused, "they all had one thing in common. When they walked into the execution room where they were to die and the chaplain asked, 'Do you have any last words?' without exception they all said the same thing. No matter how hard they had been, every one of them said, 'Yes, Sir, I would like to pray.'" Then he concluded, "We have never executed an atheist in the state of Texas."

Atheism, I am convinced, is more of the lip than of the heart. The atheist can't find God for the same reason a thief can't find a policeman—he doesn't want to. People deny God because they want to live like the devil, and that's comfortable for them.

But deep down inside I believe we all know that God is and that ultimately we must face Him. No lesser intellect than H. G. Wells, one of the greatest historians who called himself an agnostic, confided, "At times in the silence of the night, and in rare lonely moments I experience a sort of communion of myself with something great that is not myself." In those lonely moments of life, in the stillness of the night, we are all aware of God. And when people are about to step out into eternity, they know that God is. One day we shall all stand before Him in judgment. To know that and not prepare for it is to play the fool.

Do you doubt there is a God? Do you sincerely question His existence? If so, there is a promise in God's Word for you. Jesus was speaking to honest doubters when He said, "My doctrine is not mine, but him that sent me. If any man will do his will, he shall know of the doctrine, whether it be of God, or whether I speak of myself" (John 7:16-17).

In plain English this says, if a person will surrender his will completely, God will reveal Himself to that person.

Are you willing to say, "God, I do not know whether or not You exist, but I want to know, and because I want to know I will make an honest investigation, and because it is an honest investigation, I will follow the results of that investigation where they lead me, regardless of the cost"?

If so, you can know God.

Don't live like a fool. Don't think like a fool. Don't die like a fool. Come to God through faith and His dear Son Jesus Christ and live intelligently.

4
The Contemporary Book
(Psalm 19)

A young man wanted a car for graduation, but instead his father gave him a Bible. When he unwrapped it, he was so disappointed he placed it on his book shelf and forgot about it. Later his father asked, "Do you read your Bible?"

"No, Sir."

"Bring it here." He opened the Bible, and a check slipped out—made out for the price of a new car. "Son," the father emphasized, "You have missed your heart's desire because you neglected to look in the Book!"

Many people miss life at its best for the same reason. The Bible is the only book through which God speaks. God has spoken in various ways: through creation, through our consciences, and through His Son Jesus Christ. But, primarily, God has spoken to us through His written revelation, the inspired Word of God. Without it we would be almost totally ignorant of spiritual matters.

This is the message of Psalm 19. The psalmist begins by declaring that God speaks to us in nature. "The heavens declare the glory of God; and the firmament [the vast expanse of space] showeth his handiwork" (v. 1).

God's message in nature goes out every day and every night, in every language, and to every land (vv. 2-3). It is like the sun. The sun is a ball of gas 864,000 miles in diameter that is always burning. It beams its light every day, to every land (v. 4). Just so, the message of God through nature is beamed every day to every land and in every language.

There is no place on the face of the earth, no matter how remote, and no people, no matter how primitive, but that God speaks to them through His creation every day.

God not only reveals Himself in nature, the psalmist said, He also reveals Himself to us in Scripture. He wrote,

> The law of the Lord is perfect, converting the soul: the testimony of the Lord is sure, making wise the simple. The statutes of the Lord are right, rejoicing the heart: the commandment of the Lord is pure, enlightening the eyes. The fear of the Lord is clean, enduring for ever: The judgments of the Lord are true and righteous altogether (vv. 7-9).

As the writer described the word of God to us, he piled line on top of line to emphasize the nature and purpose of God's Word to show us how important it is to our lives.

Then in the next verse he said that the Word of God is more valuable than gold and sweeter than honey. These are but two of the more than one dozen analogies found in Scripture to describe the Word of God to us.

Because God's Word is so important, we need to take a brand-new look at the grand old Book. One of the best ways is to look at some of the symbols used to describe it. In this chapter we will examine five. We will see that the Word of God is food to nourish us; light to guide us; a mirror to reveal us; a seed to energize us; and a sword to expose us.

Don't Be a Junkie

The favorite symbol of the Holy Spirit to describe the Word of God is food. Peter spoke of God's word as milk for a baby (1 Pet. 2:2). Paul and the writer of Hebrews called it meat for mature men (Heb. 5:13; 1 Cor. 3:2). The psalmist told us that it is sweeter than honey (Ps. 19:10; 119:103). And Jesus compares it to bread (Matt. 4:4). Meat and milk, bread and honey—that's not a bad diet!

When Jesus said, "Man shall not live by bread alone, but by every word that proceedeth out of the mouth of God" (Matt. 4:4), He was recognizing that there was something in us that cannot be satisfied by meat and potatoes alone. There is a spiritual side to us that must be nurtured by the Word of God. Just as we must have food for our bodies, so we must have nourishment for our spirits. As meat and milk, bread and honey nourish, strengthen, and sustain the physical body, so the Word of God nourishes, strengthens, and sustains our spirits.

We hear a great deal today about world hunger. One third of the people on our planet struggle just to get enough to eat every day. Many of them do not make it; Ten thousand, in fact, die of starvation every day.

But there is another kind of famine that does not seem to bother people. Amos spoke of a coming famine, not of bread or of water, "but of hearing the words of the Lord" (Amos 8:11-13). And as a result, he wrote, young men and young women would faint in the difficult task of living because they lack the inner strength to stand up to life.

We are seeing the results of that kind of spiritual starvation all around us today. When young people eat junk food, read junk books, watch junk movies, and listen to junk music, they grow up to be moral and spiritual junkies. And instead of having the strength of character to stand up to life, they try to escape from it through alcohol, drugs, and the ultimate escape—suicide. Outer pressures without inner braces result in collapsed lives every time.

While it is necessary for us to earnestly contend for the faith once delivered to the saints, we must at the same time feed on the word of God. Wrote Dr. W. Graham Scroggie in 1930, "Bread is baked not for an analysis, but for consumption." We must avoid the temptation to argue about the menu and avoid the meal. The need of the hour is not so much to discuss the recipe as to break the bread and pass it out to the hungry multitudes. All of us face the danger of neglecting a proper spiritual diet. It is all too possible even for God's soldiers to be starving.

There is danger that we shall pore over the cookbook and never taste the Bread of Life ourselves. If God's people are to know Him, be strong, and do great works, they must stop discussing God's Word and start devouring it.

We may believe in the verbal inspiration of the Bible but receive no vital inspiration from its pages. We may believe in the inerrancy of the Bible but not allow it to correct us in our error. We may believe in the authority of God's Word in the abstract but never come practically under its authority. That is the tragedy of a dead orthodoxy, an empty evangelicalism, a fruitless fundamentalism.

It is no new problem that we face. At various times Christians have majored on the fundamentals of the faith and minored on the fruits of the Spirit. God's Word was not given to supply fuel for the fires of controversy, but food for the soul. Soldiers in the battle stop awhile and feast on the Word. We must have it if we are going to be nourished and strengthened for the difficult task of living victoriously.

Light for the Darkness

The Bible is also described as a light to guide us. The psalmist said, "Thy word is a lamp unto my feet, and a light unto my path" (Ps. 119:105). Our present world is in darkness. It is ruled over by the prince of the power of darkness (Col. 1:13; Eph. 6:12). He has thus blinded the eyes and confused the minds of people so they do not know the truth and have lost their sense of direction. Never has our nation been more susceptible to the occult, Eastern religions, and sects as it is today.

What makes this so amazing is the fact that we are living in a time of increased enlightenment in almost every other area of life. John Naisbitt, in his best-selling book *Megatrends,* pointed out that we are moving from the industrial society to the information society. Almost all the people currently being added to the job market are involved in some way with the collecting, arranging, and disbursing of information.

We are experiencing an information explosion unparalleled in history. Between six- and seven-thousand scientific articles are written each day. Scientific and technical information now increases 13 percent per year, which means it doubles every 5.5 years.

But the rate will soon jump to 40 percent per year because of new, more powerful information systems and an increasing population of scientists. That means that data will double every twenty months. In the next few years the volume of information will be somewhere between four and seven times what it was only a few years ago.

I can pick up only ten channels on my television set at the present, but soon, I am told, I will be able to choose from as many as one-hundred channels. If that becomes a reality the next generation of young people will have eyes the size of saucers and brains the size of split peas.

But don't be misled by all of this enlightment. We are drowning in information, but we are starved for knowledge and wisdom. We have better houses but worse homes. We travel at a faster speed but with less sense of direction. We enjoy more freedom but exercise less restraint. We have more luxuries but experience more misery than any previous generation.

It matters not how far we travel into outer space or how complicated our computers become—without this Book we stumble in spiritual darkness.

Paul tells us that God has given us His Word to teach us what to believe, to point out error in our lives; to give us a new sense of direction; and to help us to become the whole and happy people we were created to be (2 Tim. 3:16-17).

Take a Good Look at Yourself

The Bible is also described as a mirror to reveal us (Jas. 1:24). As we look into it carefully and prayerfully, it reveals our true character to us; it shows us our true selves.

Mirrors are tremendously important to us. In fact, I dare say, one of the first things you did this morning was look into a mirror. You wanted to assess the damage of the night before and begin a program of reconstruction. So, we look into mirrors to wash our faces, brush our teeth, shave our beards, and blow-dry our hair. And when we finish, we not only feel like new people, we may look like it.

Can you imagine growing up in a society without mirrors, living your life without ever seeing yourself? I have been in places where that was true. Several years ago I went to Belize, Central America, on a mission trip. A

British Air Force helicopter flew us deep into the jungle and into a Maya Indian village. It was like being taken back fifteen hundred years in history. The people lived in thatched huts with dirt floors and cooked over open fires in the center of their huts. About the only material possessions they had were the clothes they wore and a few pots and pans they had bought from peddlers who occasionally traveled through the jungle, bearing their wares on their backs. Mirrors were unheard of among them. Most of them had never seen themselves except as a reflection in the river.

One of the most memorable things about our trip was that we had a Polaroid camera. While Dr. Kerfoot Walker treated the villagers medically, I entertained the children by taking Polaroid shots of them. They watched with utter amazement as the pictures developed before their eyes. They, of course, recognized their friends in the pictures because they had seen them all their lives. Then, slowly, it would dawn upon them that they were also looking at a picture of themselves. They would look at the picture and then look down at their clothing, look back at the picture, and back at their clothing again. Then broad smiles would come across their faces as they realized they were looking at their own pictures.

Imagine growing up never having seen yourself in a mirror or in a photograph—not really knowing what you look like. What's worse is that many people grow up and never see themselves as God sees them. They never get a real glimpse of their character, of their true selves. The function of the Word of God is to be a mirror. The mirror reflects us exactly as we are. When we honestly read the Bible, we see not only a portrait of the "other man," we look into a mirror and see ourselves. The Bible shows men precisely what they are.

But let me warn you, if you begin to read the Bible, you may be surprised at what you see of yourself. You may be like the man who was talking to a preacher once and confessed, "Preacher, I have just one fault; I cuss a little when I get drunk." He had more faults than he realized. You may discover the same about yourself.

I remind you that a mirror is intended to improve us, not to approve of us. Some people use mirrors merely to admire themselves, but most of us use them to change ourselves. The purpose of looking into the Bible is not to find justification for our conduct but rather to find help in the right kind of living. The purpose is to practice what we read. Through practice we become mature.

There are many people cruising from church to church, from Bible conference to Bible conference, filling notebook after notebook, wearing out Bible after Bible, who are still some of the crankiest, fussiest, most judgmental, and most irresponsible people you meet. Why? Because they do not practice what they hear. Practicing what you hear is how to become mature. It is one thing to grow old in the Lord; it is another thing to grow up in the Lord. A mature person is one who is involved in practicing on a regular, consistent basis what he hears and what he reads from the Word of God. Simply being exposed to Bible instruction won't solve the problem.

Tremendous Potential for Growth

The Bible is also called a seed to energize us. Jesus once told the parable of the sower in which He compared the word of God to a seed that could reproduce itself a hundredfold (Matt. 13:1-23). Seeds are tremendously important to all of life. Did you know that all the flowers, all the fruit, and all the trees of all the tomorrows are found in the seeds of today? Seeds are the source of survival for their species. Seeds are the promise of tomorrow. Destroy all of the seeds of today, and you have destroyed all plant life for tomorrow.

A seed's power of growth is all but infinite. Jesus talked about a seed producing a hundredfold. Now those of you who know anything about farming will realize that for a bushel of corn to produce only a hundredfold would be a meager yield. Corn planted on good ground will produce far more. But, assuming that corn produces only a hundredfold, suppose you had one bushel of corn and were to plant it and its product for so brief a period as fifteen years, how much corn would you have? Those of you who still remember your geometric progression can quickly find the answer.

At the end of the first year you would have one hundred bushels, at the end of the second, ten thousand bushels, at the end of the third, one million bushels. At the end of the fifteen years you would have enough corn that if it were rolled into popcorn balls it would make 31,536,188 worlds the size of ours, with a fraction left over! That small fraction left over, we are told, would be enough to feed the present population of the earth for a thousand years. Such is the might of growing power in the vegetable kingdom.

Seeds not only have the power to reproduce but to overcome. Sometime ago we built a parking lot at our church. We bought several old houses and moved them to provide parking space. First we dug up the topsoil and replaced it with iron-ore gravel. Then we repeatedly graded, watered, and rolled the gravel until it was packed as hard as concrete. Then the contractors placed four inches of hot asphalt on top of that iron-ore base.

Not many months after the project was completed, I was walking across the parking lot, and what should I see but a tiny blade of grass poking through that asphalt?

What had happened? Down deep beneath the surface there had been a seed. In spite of all of the pounding, abuse, and the thick layer of asphalt above it, the little seed had taken off its coat through germination and pushed and shoved its way out into the sunlight. Given enough time and allowed to grow unchecked, that single seed would eventually take over the entire parking lot. Such is the multiplying and overcoming power of a seed.

A seed may lie dormant for a long time before it ever sprouts into growth. I read recently that an archeologist digging in an ancient Egyptian tomb found a bowl of seeds over three thousand years old—when planted they sprouted and grew!

The Word of God is like that. It has tremendous multiplying and overcoming power if it is planted in human hearts. So don't be weary in well-doing. Keep planting God's Word wherever you can, and though there may be a long delay, growth and life will eventually come. Many people become discouraged because they don't not see immediate results. Remember, when God wants to grow an oak tree He takes a hundred years. When He wants to grow a squash He takes only three months.

We are to plant and to water, but God gives the increase. He has promised that His word will not return unto Him void (Isa. 55:10-11).

Do You Need an Analyst?

Finally, the Bible is compared to a knife that exposes our inmost being. The writer of Hebrews said,

> For the word of God is quick, and powerful, and sharper than any two-edged sword, piercing even to the dividing asunder of soul and spirit, and of the joints and marrow,

and is a discerner of the thoughts and intents of the heart (Heb. 4:12).

The Bible is called a two-edged sword because it cuts coming and going. As a sword used in battle can rip a person open and reveal his inner parts, so the Word of God is like a surgeon's scalpel that exposes our insides.

The writer described the word of God as a "discerner" of the thoughts and intents of our hearts. The word *discern* means to sift, to analyze, to expose. It is like an analyst who reveals our inner thoughts, our private ambitions, our jealousies, our unspiritual vulgarity, our false conclusions, and our temper of rebellion.

We live in a day of analysts. There are chemical, computer, political, financial, and psycho analysts. But the analyst we need most of all is the Word of God.

Smiley Blanton, a Christian psychiatrist who died recently, wrote that once a new patient noticed the Bible lying on his desk. "Do you, a psychiatrist, read the Bible?" the patient asked.

"I not only read it," Blanton told him, "I study it. It's the greatest textbook on human behavior ever put together. If people would just absorb its message, a lot of us psychiatrists could close our offices and go fishing."

Many people today trying to get adjusted need to get converted. They are trying to have their sins explained when they need to have them forgiven.

Somebody has aptly said, "If you ever see a Bible that's falling apart, it usually belongs to a person who isn't." Let the Word of God analyze you, and you will have little need of other analysts.

As Jesus closed the Sermon on the Mount He stated, "Whosoever heareth these sayings of mine, and doeth them, I will liken him unto a wise man, which built his house upon a rock" (Matt. 7:24). God's Word is the only lasting foundation there is. It alone can stand the test of time and trials. Build your life on it. Build your marriage and home on it. Build your business on it. Build your ministry and class on it. It is the only lasting way to the life worth living.

5
"He's All I Want"
(Psalm 23)

A little girl announced that she was going to draw a picture of God. Her mother objected, "Why, no one knows what God looks like." The little girl replied, "They will when I get through."

The Twenty-third Psalm is a word picture of God. When David got through with it, we have a better idea of what God is like.

His opening statement, "The Lord is my shepherd," is the key to the whole psalm.

The word "Lord" is the Hebrew name "Yahweh." It is the personal name for God that distinguished Him from all the false gods of that day. It is the most popular name for God in the Bible, being used 6,823 times in Scripture. The name was so revered by the ancient Jews that it was never spoken, only written. When they spoke the name of God they used the title "Adonai." And when they wrote the name *Yahweh*, each time they did it with a new quill and new ink. If a scribe, in the process of copying the Scriptures, came to the name Yahweh, he and found new materials that had never been used before. Then with new pen and new ink he wrote "Yahweh." Each time thereafter he went through the same process.

If the ancient Jews went to extremes in one direction with the name of God, our generation has gone to extremes in the other. This generation uses the name of God so carelessly that it means virtually nothing.

The verb "is" is in the present tense. In fact, every verb in this psalm is in the present tense. David was not telling us what God had done for him in the past or what he hoped God would do for him in the future. Rather, he was telling what God meant to him *right at that moment.*

What is your present-tense testimony about God? If you were called upon to testify for the Lord, would you have to go back to your childhood to speak of His working in your life? What does He mean to you *now? Today?*

David used the personal pronoun "my." He did not say the Lord is *a* shepherd (that is, one among many). Nor did he say the Lord is *the* shepherd as though He were distant and remote. David said, "[He] is my shepherd." Everything wears a different look when we can speak of it as our very own. It is one thing to say, "There is a baby." It is something else to say, "There is *my* baby." It is one thing to say, "There is a home." It is something entirely different to say, "There is *my* home."

Many people talk about God in generalities but are reluctant to become personal about Him. To profess intimacy with Him is, to them, an embarrassment. However, our experience with God can never be vital until it is personal.

Perhaps you have heard the old story of two men who were called on to recite the Twenty-third Psalm. One was an actor trained in speech technique and drama. He repeated the psalm dynamically. The audience cheered. Then the other, an older man, repeated the same words, "The Lord is my shepherd; I shall not want . . . ." When he finished, there was not a sound. Instead, the people sat quietly in devotion and awe.

The actor arose and explained, "The difference between what you have just heard from this elderly gentleman and what you have heard from me is this: I know the Psalm; he knows the Shepherd."

The word *shepherd* suggests God's tender care. David had been a shepherd as a lad. He understood what it was to lead his sheep, to protect them from danger, to seek after them when they went astray, to anoint them with oil when they were wounded, and then to bring them safely into the fold at the end of the day. From his own experience he declared: "The Lord is to me what a shepherd is to his sheep."

With this awareness of God it naturally follows that David would add, "I shall not want." God is all-sufficient, supplying our every need. A little girl put it this way, "The Lord is my shepherd. He is all I want."

David touched almost every aspect of life as he completed this portrait of God's marvelous provision. An unknown poet wrote:

> For our weariness, there are green pastures;
> For our anxieties, there is still water;
> For our falterings, there is restoration;
> For our perplexities, there is guidance;
> For our fears, there is comfort;
> For our enemies, there is a feast;
> For our hurts, there is anointing;
> For the end, there is the Father's house.

God is our all-sufficient, ever-present, fully satisfying Shepherd.

He Is All-Sufficient

A good friend recently went through a profound emotional crisis, which also resulted in a financial crisis. He testified to me, "It's wonderful to see how God is meeting my need." I asked him, "Don't you suppose God has been meeting your needs all along and you simply haven't aware of it?" And he replied, "Yes, I think that's it."

God does meet our needs day by day, but we are often unaware of it. All of life comes from God, including your life. God who cares for the birds of the air and the lillies of the field also cares for you.

Notice how David described God's all-sufficiency: "He maketh me to lie down in green pastures" (v. 2). It is almost impossible to make sheep lie down while they are hungry. They will mill around and nibble on bits of grass here and there until they have eaten sufficiently. Only when their stomachs are full will they find a quiet place and lie down. Sheep lying down in green pastures is a picture of contentment and satisfaction.

Contentment is a missing ingredient in our society. This is a day of pervading dissatisfaction. We are under constant pressure to stay up or to "get ahead," to be a success. As an unknown wag put it, "We spend money we don't have to buy things we don't need to keep up with people we don't like." Through our discontentment we produce phobias, ulcers, and anxieties.

Most people can never say with the apostle Paul, ". . . I have learned in whatsoever state I am, therewith to be content" (Phil. 4:11). That is because they do not believe that "God shall supply all of their needs according to his riches in glory by Christ Jesus" (v. 19). Only the person who has confidence in the provision of God can be content in this life.

"He leadeth me beside the still waters," sang David. Sheep will not drink from swiftly running water for a good reason. They are poor swimmers. If their wool coats become soaked with water the weight will pull them under. It would be like trying to swim wearing an overcoat.

Instinctively, sheep know this, and so they will not go near swiftly running water. If the shepherd cannot find still water, he must build a small dam with stones at the edge of the stream. Otherwise, his sheep will be afraid to drink.

Sheep beside still waters is a picture of peace and rest. The words "still waters" literally mean "waters of rest." When the storms of life come, regardless of their origin, the Lord is able to speak "Peace be still" to the winds and the waves. As our Lord calmed the Sea of Galilee in the days of old, so He can still the turbulence of our lives today.

This picture reminds us of the words of Jesus, "Come unto me, all ye that labour and are heavy laden, and I will give you rest. Take my yoke upon you, and learn of me; for I am meek and lowly in heart: and ye shall find rest unto your souls, For my yoke is easy, and my burden is light" (Matt. 11:28-30).

"He restoreth my soul." Sheep are not very smart. They have a predictable inclination to lose their way. They can be in a pasture with plenty of grass and adequate water and still wander aimlessly until they have nothing to eat or drink. Once lost, they can't find their way back. There are instances of cats and dogs going more than two thousand miles to find their way home. Many animals seem to have inborn compasses—not so with sheep. Once lost, the shepherds must go and find them.

Spiritually, people are like sheep. Isaiah the prophet wrote, "All we, like sheep, have gone astray" (Isa. 53:6). I once saw a cartoon that pictured two sheep grazing in a pasture. One commented to the other, "All we, like people, have gone astray." Sheep are like people. People are like sheep. Both are easily lost.

We have a profound tendency to desert whatever is good for us. The grass always looks greener on the other side of the fence. So we often go away from God into sin. When we do, the Lord, "restoreth our soul." The word *restore* literally means "to bring back, to renew, to revive." It describes how God seeks to bring us back to Himself when we wander away.

David was probably rethinking the darkest, most tragic crisis of his own life—when he committed adultery and then tried to cover his wrong by murder. David's life was in the pits until God sent Nathan, the prophet, to call him to repentance and to a restored relationship.

Only God can restore our soul in this sense. Dr. R. B. Robins, speaking to a large number of physicians, once noted, "The psychiatrist's couch cannot take the place of the church in solving the problems of a frustrated society."

"He leadeth me in the paths of righteousness for his name's sake." Sheep have poor eyesight. They cannot see more than fifteen yards ahead of them. So, they need to be led. I read once in the newspaper of a mass death leap of 1,050 sheep over a cliff in the Alpine region of France. The sheep were obviously frightened by other animals, and, shoulder-to-shoulder, surged over a cliff to their destruction. Their lack of sight led to their destruction. Sheep need a shepherd.

Like sheep, we also need guidance. We often come to crossroads in our lives and don't know where to turn or what to do. Fear of making the wrong decision paralyzes many people. They want to know right and to do right, but they are unsure of themselves. The result is that counselors, advisers, and gurus do a landslide business. In seeking counsel and advice we must not overlook "the" Shepherd.

The Scriptures promise, "Trust in the Lord with all thine heart; and lean not unto thine own understanding.

In all thy ways acknowledge him, and he shall direct thy paths" (Prov. 3:5-6). And again, "If any of you lack wisdom, let him ask of God, that giveth to all men liberally, and upbraideth not; and it shall be given him" (Jas. 1:5).

The word "righteousness" is used here in a moral sense. Put yourself under the direction of the Shepherd; follow Him, and He will direct you in the right paths of life.

He will do it for your sake and "for His name's sake." God's name and character are at stake in us. We should live holy lives to His everlasting honor and glory.

He Is Ever Present

David's emphasis upon God's provision intensifies as he sang, "Yea, though I walk through the valley of the shadow of death, I will fear no evil: for thou art with me: thy rod and thy staff, they comfort me" (v. 4).

The "valley of the shadow" literally means "a place of deep gloom" or "black darkness." It may refer to death, although it should not be limited to that. It encompasses any of the dark, gloomy, dreadful experiences of life.

We do not have to live long before we realize that life is not all "green pastures" and "still waters." The green pastures can become jagged peaks. The still waters can become turbulent seas. Even being one of God's children does not exempt us from the valleys of dark gloom. Christians contract cancer. Christians have accidents. Christians suffer financial reversals.

When life tumbles in, what then? We still have the Shepherd. The difference in the child of God and in others is not the absence of shadows; it is the presence of the Shepherd.

Listening to a student read this Scripture in seminary chapel, Joseph Sittler, now blind, heard something he'd never heard before. "Yea, though I walk through the valley of the shadow of death, I will fear no evil: for thou art with me."

Sittler said;

> The text does not speak of the valley of death but of the valley of the shadow of death. There is a difference . . . . The wonderful truth . . . is that God is with us now. It is not simply that God will be with us in the experience of death itself; it is that God will walk with us through all of life, a life over which death sometimes casts its shadow.[1]

Alexander Maclaren told about the time he accepted his first job in Glasgow, Scotland. He was only sixteen and his home was about six miles from the big city. Between his home and Glasgow was a deep ravine that was supposedly haunted. Some terrible happenings had reportedly occurred in it throughout the years. He was afraid to go through in the daytime. At night, it was unthinkable.

On Monday morning his father walked with him to work and in parting instructed, "Alec, come home as fast as you can when you get off Saturday night."

Thinking of that dark ravine, Maclaren answered him with, "Father, I'll be awfully tired Saturday night. I'll come home early Sunday morning."

But his father was insistent, "No, Alec, you have never been away from home before, and these five days are going to seem like a year to me. Come home Saturday night."

He reluctantly answered, "All right, Father, Saturday night."

All week long, Alec said, he worried about that black ravine. When Saturday night came, he was more scared than ever, but he wrapped up his belongings and walked out to the end of the gulch. He reported, "I whistled to keep up my courage, but when I looked down into the empty blackness I knew I could not go on. Big tears came unbidden. Then, suddenly, I heard footsteps in the ravine coming up the path. I started to run but hesitated because those footsteps were very familiar.

"Up out of the darkness and into the pale light as I watched, came the head and the shoulders of the grandest man on earth. He was bound to have known that I was scared, but he only said, 'Alec, I wanted to see you so badly that I came to meet you.' So shoulder to shoulder we went down into the valley, and I was not afraid of anything that walked."

When the time comes to walk through the valley of the shadow of death, or any other gloomy experience, we can have the same calm assurance, for the Lord is with us. We are not alone.

He Fully Satisfies

David concluded the psalm by saying,

Thou preparest a table before me in the presence of mine enemies: thou anointest my head with oil; my cup runneth over. Surely goodness and mercy shall follow me all the days of my life: and I will dwell in the house of the Lord for ever (vv. 5-6).

With these verses the image of the psalm suddenly changes. We are no longer in a field but in a palace. The Lord is no longer the Good Shepherd; He is now a gracious host. He prepares a table, He pours a cup, and He dwells in His house forever. What have tables, cups, and a house to do with a shepherd?

For years I wondered myself. Then last year in Israel I learned the answer. There is an ancient desert custom among the Bedouin sheikhs going back to David's time. According to the custom, the sheikh must invite any wanderer who passes his tent to be his guest for up to three days. At the end of this time, the sheikh accompanies the traveler to the border of his territory and is no longer responsible for him.

In contrast to the temporary provision of these shepherds, there is the eternal provision of the "Good Shepherd."

These words clearly go beyond earth to eternity. They speak of God's eternal provision. There are some things in life for sure. This is one of them. "I will dwell in the house of the Lord for ever." The word "dwell" means "to settle down and be at home." When we come to the end of this life, there is the Father's house awaiting us.

When David penned these words he was an old man. He had experienced tragedy, disappointment, heartaches, and hurts. He had come to know the Lord as his Shepherd, and he now lived with confidence and calm assurance in Him.

So can we. Look at it from the standpoint of an anonymous poet:

> Beneath us . . . green pastures.
> Beside us . . . still waters.
> With us . . . his rod and staff.
> Before us . . . a table.
> Around us . . . our enemies.
> After us . . . goodness and mercy.
> Ahead of us . . . the house of the Lord.
> Hallelujah? What a Saviour and a Shepherd!

Can you say with David, "The Lord is my shepherd " The Lord will not be your shepherd until you make Him your Savior.

Jesus said, "I am the good shepherd. . . . I lay down my life for the sheep" (John 10:14-15). Christ died that He might bring us back to God. He arose from the grave and now has become "the Shepherd and Bishop of your souls" (1 Pet. 2:25). Come to the Good Shepherd, Jesus Christ, today. Then you can affirm with David, "The Lord is my shepherd, I shall not want—in life or in death or in eternity."

NOTE

1. Quoted by Martin Marty in *Context*, August 1 and 15, 1984.

6
"Oh, What a Relief It Is!"
(Psalm 32)

"Oh, what a relief it is!" went a television commercial. The psalmist said a similar tune. The commercial was singing about a digestive disorder, only the psalmist was vocalizing about the forgiveness of sins.

The essence of these words was spoken by David in Psalm 32. This psalm is a sequel to Psalm 51 in which he confessed his sin of adultery with Bathsheba. Here he described the blessings that came with the forgiveness of that sin which followed chastening and confession (vv. 1-5). Then he encouraged us always to seek the Lord's deliverance rather than stubbornly refuse to follow Him (vv. 6-10). And finally, he extolled us to rejoice in the Lord (v. 11).

The psalm begins, "Blessed is he whose transgression is forgiven." The word *blessed* means "incredibly happy." In the statement that follows, David uses four words to describe the wrong he had done: "transgression," "sin," "iniquity," and "guile."

The word *transgress* means "to do what is forbidden"; the word *sin* means "to fail to do what is required"; the word *iniquity* means "to pervert that which is good"; the word *guile* means "to project what is false."

We have been guilty of transgressions, sins, iniquities, and guile. I will discuss the first three in chapter 8. Now look at that word *guile*. Culture demands a certain amount of guile from every one of us. For example, we often greet people, "Hello, how are you doing today?" when we really may not care how they are doing. It is merely one of the cultural niceties of life.

Like most pastors, I make a practice of standing at the front door of the church at the close of our worship services to greet the people as they leave. In one church I pastored, I had a member who was a hypochondriac. She delighted in telling everyone about her infirmities. When I greeted her, "Hello, how are you today?" she always stopped and told me, and it was always bad. I soon learned how to deal with her. When I saw her approaching, I would put a broad smile on my face, take her by the hand and pull her gently past me, remarking all the while, "My, you sure look good today."

In both instances I was projecting falsity. I was a hypocrite to a hypochondriac. Some of that is simply a part of life, but the real problem comes when we express false feelings to God. That's what David had done. He had been playing the hypocrite before both God and man.

For more than a year David expended a tremendous amount of emotional energy trying to cover up his sin. Inwardly, it was tearing him apart. David faced the tension between the need to conceal and the need to reveal his sin. He confessed, "When I declared not my sin my body wasted away" (vv. 3-4, RSV). David's sin was having a devastating effect upon him. He was growing old before his time, under intense emotional pressure, and losing his vitality.

Physically, emotionally, and spiritually David was suffering. Guilt affects the whole person—ask any physician or Christian psychiatrist.

When David was confronted by Nathan the prophet, he

realized there was no longer any use in pretending. He could now cease his hypocrisy. That's when he acknowledged his sin and stopped trying to hide his past.

When David confessed his sin, he experienced the forgiveness and cleansing that he described in the beginning of this psalm. David used three words, each with a different shade of meaning to show how wonderfully and completely God dealt with his sin: "forgive," "cover," and "impute."

The word *forgive* means "to lift, to take away." When David confessed his sin it was as if a massive weight had been lifted from his shoulders. The word *cover* means "to hide." His sin was haunting him no longer. It was as if God had placed a covering over it. The word *impute* means "to cancel a debt." God erased the marks against David from the ledger of life when he confessed his sin. He was held accountable for them no longer. He was forgiven!

As David suddenly realized that he was forgiven, that he could stop pretending, that the great burden of guilt had been lifted from him, he might have cried out, "Oh, what a relief it is."

Having described for us the incredible joy that comes from forgiveness, David sought to encourage us to learn from his experience. Someone has remarked, "A fool learns from his own mistakes. Wise men learn from the mistakes of others." David wanted us to learn from his mistakes.

There are three lessons for us in the remainder of this psalm.

God Is On to Us

Lesson One: If we will confess to the Lord, He will forgive us (vv. 6-7). This truth is out of the crucible of David's own experience. He learned the hard way not to try to conceal his sin. He urged us to confess quickly and forsake our wrong so God can forgive us.

The first consciousness of sin should lead to the confession of sin. The tendency is to cover, to conceal our sin. The Scriptures warn, "He that covereth his sins shall not prosper: but whoso confesseth and forsaketh them shall have mercy" (Prov. 28:13).

Before God will forgive us of our sins and deliver us from them, we must not deceive ourselves. Self-deception about our own sinfulness is one of life's most common mistakes (1 John 1:10).

Augustine said, "The beginning of wisdom is to know yourself to be a sinner." Only when we face up to our own wrongdoing will God forgive and remove it.

When you confess to God, you don't pass on to Him information He didn't have before. God has been "on to" you and me for a long time. He simply wants us to realize our wrong, be sorry for it, and turn from it.

Don't Be Like a Donkey

Lesson Two: Obey the Lord, and He will lead you (vv. 8-9). The Lord wants to lead us "in the paths of righteousness" (Ps. 23:3). He does not want to drive us to righteousness but to lead us gently "with His eye." Eyes can be very expressive. They can "speak" many messages to us.

For example, you can roll your eyes back as if to say "Oh, no!" You can cut them first to one side and then the other as if to say, "Is anybody listening?" You can open them wide as if to say "Watch out!" Or you can wink and communicate all kinds of nuances.

While God seeks to lead us gently, we do not have to follow Him. We can stubbornly refuse to obey. David urged in this psalm, "Be ye not as the horse, or as the mule, which have no understanding" (v. 9*a*).

It is an interesting study to see how often God uses animals in the Bible to teach us. He says, "Go to the ant, thou sluggard; consider her ways" (Prov. 6:6). An ant is an example of industry, of hard work. Ants can lift fifty times their own weight. If I could do that, I could lift nine thousand pounds. And ants work tirelessly. We are told to learn from the rabbit who, though feeble, builds his home in the rocks. The rabbit, being weak and defenseless against larger and more vicious animals, must use wisdom in building his home in a safe place. The rabbit is held up for us as an example of wisdom.

Jesus said, "Behold the fowls of the air" (Matt. 6:26). The birds teach us to trust God for our daily bread. He advises, "Be ye therefore wise as serpents, and harmless as doves" (Matt. 10:16).

In this passage we are told not to be like a mule. What trait does a mule most commonly characterize? Stubborness. We are here warned against stubbornly refusing to obey the Lord.

One of my heroes is the late Amos Alonzo Stagg. He coached at the University of Chicago until he was seventy years of age. Then he moved to The College of the Pacific where he coached for another fourteen years—until he was eighty-four years old. Eddie LeBaron, the first quarterback of the Dallas Cowboys, was the last All-American to play under Coach Stagg. When Coach Stagg retired from The College of the Pacific, he joined his son's coaching staff for another six years—until he was ninety. Then he coached one more year, as a junior college assistant, finally retiring at the age of ninety-one.

Early in his life, Stagg, a devout Presbyterian, felt called into the ministry, but feeling that he was unsuited for the pulpit, he went into coaching. He said, "My ministry is the young men of America."

"Oh, What a Relief It Is!"

As a Christian, Coach Stagg never used profanity. The worst word he ever used was *jackass*. If a player messed up he would call him that. If he really messed up he would call him a "double jackass." If he did really, really badly, he called him a "triple jackass." When there was extreme provocation he would call the unfortunate "the king of the jackasses."

His players said, "He never left the practice field with humans on it. He always left the entire squad grazing."

Sarah Churchill told in her book *Keep on Dancing* that her father Winston once commented to her that we had, to a large extent, succeeded in the civilized world in erasing the lion and the tiger from the human soul. But we had not succeeded in removing the donkey.

What about you? All of us are occasionally accused of acting like a donkey. Sometimes the charges are justified. How are we to respond to them? Someone put it like this: Solitary shots should be ignored, but when they come from several directions, it's time to pay attention. If one person calls you a donkey, ignore him. If two call you a donkey, check for hoofprints. If three call you a donkey, find a saddle!

David's warning was: "Don't have a stubborn and rebellious spirit. Don't force God to drive you and chasten you into doing what is right. Respond to him, follow Him, and He will 'guide you with his eye.'"

Solomon, David's son, expressed the same truth: "Trust in the Lord with all thine heart; and lean not unto thine own understanding. In all thy ways acknowledge him, and he shall direct thy paths" (Prov. 3:5-6).

The Way to Blessings

Lesson Three: Trust in the Lord and He will bless you (v. 10). David declared that the wicked have many sorrows. The writer of Proverbs agreed. He told us, "The way of transgressors is hard" (13:15).

Robert Louis Stevenson in his book, *The Case of Dr. Jekyll and Mr. Hyde*, had Hyde say, "If I am the chief of sinners, I am also the chief of sufferers."

Sin brings sorrow, but trust in the Lord brings mercy. David was a living example of this.

He closed by exhorting, "Be glad in the Lord, and rejoice, ye righteous: and shout for joy, all ye that are upright in heart" (v. 11).

Years ago a man was sharing his conversion experience with me. As he told me about the former pastor who had led him to Christ, he said, "He taught me two great lessons in life. First, the Christian life is fun. Second, the Christian life is hard."

This is one of the paradoxes of the Christian life. It is a mixture of agony and ecstasy. There are struggles and hardships, temptations and trials. But there is also the incredible joy of forgiveness and the intimacy of fellowship with God. This is what David had experienced and also what he wanted us to experience.

David wrote this psalm as a model of what might also happen in your life. We know from our vantage point that the forgiveness he described here has been made possible through the death of Jesus upon the cross. He died that the weight of sin and guilt might be lifted from our shoulders. His blood becomes a covering for our sins. He died in our place and thus paid the debt for us. Through faith and trust in Him, the forgiveness and the joy David described can be yours now.

7
Lessons of Life and Death
(Psalm 39)

"Death," said Robert M. Herhold, "is that final separation from all that we have worked for, and that we have built up, and that is near and dear to us. It is too bad that dying is the last thing we do. Because it could teach us so much about living."

We may learn many lessons from death. The psalmist wrote about some of them,

> Lord, make me know mine end, and the measure of my days, what it is; that I may know how frail I am. Behold thou hast made my days as a handbreadth; and mine age is as nothing before thee: verily every man at his best state is altogether vanity. Selah. Surely every man walketh in a vain shew: surely they are disquieted in vain: he heapeth up riches, and knoweth not who shall gather them. And now, Lord, what wait I for? my hope is in thee (Ps. 39:4-7).

When David penned these words he was bowed down by distress and sorrow. The chastening hand of God weighed heavily upon him (v. 10). In his sorrow he was tempted to complain against God about his harrowing experiences. Instead, he manifested self-control and began to think about the brevity of life and the certainty of death. Then he asked God to make him keenly aware of his life's frailty, so he might make the most of it.

In these verses we need to know the meanings of two words, in order to understand this message. The first is *handbreadth*. It was a unit of measure used in ancient days—about four inches wide, the approximate width of a man's hand. Nine of them would make a yard. In days before rulers and yardsticks were readily available, measurements were approximated by hands or feet. The word used here suggests the brevity of life.

The second word is *vanity*. It means "as a breath." James asked, "What is your life?" Then he answered, "It is even a vapour, that appeareth for a little time, and then vanisheth away" (Jas. 4:14). James conveys the same idea about the brevity and frailty of life expressed by this word.

Three times in these four verses he used the word *vain* or *vanity* to describe human frailty. He said: "Every man at his best state is altogether vanity (v. 5). Every man walketh in a vain show: surely they are disquieted in vain" (v. 6).

Then he added in verse 11: "Surely every man is vanity."

I want you to notice how vividly he expressed this truth: "Verily every man at his best state is altogether vanity" (v. 5). Take a man in the prime of life, one who eats well, has an adequate amount of rest, and plenty of exercise so his body is in top shape; even then his life is like a breath—fleeting and uncertain.

A life is as a whispering breeze and a drifting fog. In the sight of God, it is only a moment.

With life so uncertain David realized it was futile to trust in wealth and to spend all of one's time accumulating material possessions for someone else to spend. Then he concluded that our only real security is in God. The truth David proclaimed is that the frailty of life and the certainty of death ought to teach us to make the most of the time we have. The very thought of death ought to teach us three important truths about life.

Have a Healthy Respect for Time

The first idea death ought to teach us is to savor time. The psalmist prayed, "Lord, make me to know mine end, and the measure of my days, what it is; that I may know how frail I am" (v. 4). Only as we look at life from the vantage point of death can we realize how important time is. Referees call time; prisoners serve time; musicians mark time; historians record time; loafers kill time; statisticians keep time. But no matter how we relate to time, the fact remains that each of us is given a limited amount. That fact alone ought to cause us to use it wisely.

People talk about saving time, but it can't be done. You can't save time; you can only savor it, enjoy it, and make the most of it.

To look at time from the end of life gives you a healthier respect for it. Shortly after he became the director of Christian education for Texas Baptists, Don Anthony learned that he had cancer and was given only three months to live. Sometime after that he returned to his alma mater, East Texas Baptist University, for homecoming activities. He was the featured speaker on that occasion. By that time he was already yellow with jaundice, drawn, and thin from massive weight loss. When the day was over he was completely exhausted. He had made the great effort because he believed so in Christian education and in the college from which he had graduated.

Commenting on the day, President Jerry Dawson said, "When a man has only sixty days to live, and he gives you one of those days, it really means something." The truth of the matter is that each of us has a very limited supply of days. We may not know how many or how few they are, but to give one of them to any person or to anything is truly significant.

How you spend your time is far more important than how you spend your money. Money mistakes can be corrected, but time is lost forever, so we had better decide what is important and give ourselves to those matters. To me, the sequence of priority in life ought to be: your time with God, your time with yourself, your time with your family, and your time with your work.

> So, take time to work; it is the price of success.
> Take time to think; it is the source of power.
> Take time to play; it is the secret to you.
> Take time to read; it is the fountain of wisdom.
> Take time to be friendly; it is the road to happiness.
> Take time to dream; it is hitching your wagon to a star.
> Take time to love; it is the highest joy in life.
> Take time to laugh; it is the music of the soul.
> Take time for God; He is the key to eternity.
> —Author Unknown

Most of all, whatever you intend to do, you had better begin doing it today. It sounds trite, but it is true: "Today is the first day of the rest of your life." It may be the last. Remembering that can help you to savor time.

No Moving Vans Behind Hearses

The second truth we ought to learn from death is the futility of trusting in things. As the psalmist contemplated the frailty of life he wrote, "Surely every man walketh in a vain shew . . . he heapeth up riches, and knoweth not who shall gather them" (v. 6).

The man who devotes his life to the accumulation of things is a fool. He shall soon come to the end of his days and leave it all behind for someone else to inherit and enjoy or to squabble over and squander.

Several years ago I was called to the bedside of a friend who had learned he had a terminal illness and only a few months to live. The night before he had taken a legal pad and listed all of his assets on it. He then confided, "It took only six pages to list everything I own. When you put things down on paper and look at them from the end of life, instead of what you thought was the middle of life, they don't amount to much." In the light of death, not only does time look different; so do things.

Jesus once asked a question we all need to ponder: "What shall it profit a man, if he shall gain the whole world, and lose his own soul? Or what shall a man give in exchange for his soul?" (Mark 8:36).

Charlemagne the Great was, at his request, buried sitting on his throne, wearing his crown, robe, and jewels. In his lap was an open Bible, and his lead finger was resting on this verse. It poses for us one of life's most important questions.

The answer is obvious. There is nothing one can give in exchange for his soul. If one gained the whole world and it cost him his soul, he would have gained nothing but would have lost everything.

It is easy to become so caught up in making a living that we fail to make a life. We can become so preoccupied with accumulating wealth that we become spiritual beggars; we can become so anchored to the earth that we lose sight of eternity.

I am reminded of the swift exchange between two well-respected Englishmen. One asked, "How is it with your soul?" His friend replied, "My soul? I have been so busy lately I had almost forgotten I had a soul."

Don't let that happen to you. You cannot control the

length of your life, but you can determine the depth of it. You can give yourself things of eternal importance.

We need to remember that we brought nothing into this world and can carry nothing out. So, it is futile to trust in things for ultimate security.

Remember the story of two men who were discussing a wealthy man's death? One asked, "How much did he leave?" The other replied, "He left it all." So will we.

The old Chinese proverb is true: There are no pockets in a shroud. The not-so-old preacher's proverb is also true: there are no moving vans behind hearses. You can't take it with you.

Death, then, teaches us the futility of trusting in wealth.

Our Hope Is in God

The third truth death ought to teach us is the necessity of faith. The psalm goes, "And now Lord, what wait I for? my hope is in thee" (v. 7). Our only real security is of the soul which comes from trusting in the Lord.

While our life here is as a breath, God is eternal. He transcends time. Only to Him can we turn for everlasting life. Our hope is in His mercy, His forgiveness, and His salvation.

As a pastor I am often in cemeteries. I recently traveled to an old country cemetery to bury a dear friend. The little community where it was located is like thousands of others—at one time alive with people. Today an isolated farmhouse punctuates the horizon here and there. The old school has long since been torn down. A little country church is still there, but no one meets in it anymore. The cemetery is overgrown and unkempt. As I walked among the tombstones and read the epitaphs, I was reminded again of the words of the psalmist: "As for man, his days are as grass: as a flower of the field, so he flourisheth. For the wind passeth over it, and it is gone; and the place thereof shall know it no more" (Ps. 103:15-16).

I was almost tempted to despair; then I remembered the words of Jesus: "I am the resurrection, and the life: he that believeth in me, though he were dead, yet shall he live: And whosoever liveth and believeth in me shall never die" (John 11:25-26).

The resurrection of Jesus keeps the grave from being our final destiny. The culmination of eternal life lies just beyond the door of death. Through the resurrection of our Lord, death has been transformed from an ending into a beginning. Through the resurrection, death has been changed from a period to a comma; from a conclusion into an introduction; from a final destination into a rest stop. Because of Him, death is not the end of the road; it is a bend in the road.

This is our God-given hope. Jesus Christ, God's Son, died for our sins. He was buried in Joseph's tomb. On the third day He was raised from the dead and now lives forevermore. Because He lives, we also shall live. Our hope and security are in Him alone.

Each time I think about my own death, I ask myself three questions to help me evaluate how well I am prepared for that day:

Am I right in my relationship with God?

Am I right in my relationship with my family, my friends, and my co-workers?

Are there relationships I need to reconcile?

Are there words I need to speak?

And am I investing myself in things that will last for eternity?

Unless our Lord returns first, I will someday die. I will have to face death, the enemy; and I will experience death, the new beginning. It cannot be prevented, but there is plenty I can do to prepare for it. Now is the time to begin healthy and earnest preparation.

The prayer of the psalmist ought to be ours: "Lord, make me know mine end, and the measure of my days, what it is; that I may know how frail I am" (v. 4).

8
Finding Forgiveness
(Psalm 51)

When Edward R. Murrow was appointed as director of the United States Information Agency by President Kennedy, he was asked by a Senate committee what he would do to counteract Communist propaganda against America. He replied, "I believe that we ought to report all the news, warts and blemishes, as well as the sunshine."

Whenever the Word of God reports on anybody, it does so with that kind of unvarnished honesty. It does not even gloss over the sins, faults, and failures of the greatest saints of God.

King David is a case in point. Though he was "a man after God's own heart," the Word of God exposes David's warts and blemishes, as well as his virtues. The best people sometimes do the worst of things, and when they do, God doesn't try to hide it from the rest of us.

In 2 Samuel David's heinous sins are exposed. He seduced another man's wife and then, to conceal his sin, arranged for her husband to be killed. Watergate was not the first government cover-up. David set the precedent a long time ago.

After all, he was the king. Who would reprimand him? No one had to. David's own witness of this experience is found in Psalm 32. "When I kept silence, my bones waxed old through my roaring all the day long. For day and night thy hand was heavy upon me: my moisture is turned into the drought of summer" (v. 4).

The Revised Standard Version puts it this way, "When I declared not my sin, my body wasted away." David's guilt affected his entire being. He suffered physically as well as emotionally and spiritually. He tried to conceal his guilt, but inwardly it was tearing him apart. Guilt almost always does that. It creates tension between the need to conceal and the need to reveal.

David went on this way for almost a year. Then the Lord sent Nathan to confront him—causing David to acknowledge his guilt and letting it out into the open, so repentance and restoration could come about.

Nathan told David a story about a rich man who had everything and a poor man who had only one ewe lamb. A traveler came to visit the wealthy man, who spared his own flock and seized the poor man's only lamb for the traveler. David's anger was kindled; his reaction was indeed human. We often hate most vigorously the evil in others that we secretly recognize in ourselves. David told Nathan that the man must pay and asked who he was. Nathan answered, "Thou art the man" (2 Sam. 12:7). What David feared most had happened: He was exposed!

His response to that exposure was one of agonizing repentance. Though his sins were not without consequences, from his repentance came deliverance. Psalm 51 is David's prayer of repentance, and Psalm 32 is his witness to the sweetness of forgiveness: "Blessed is he whose transgression is forgiven, whose sin is covered. Blessed is the man unto whom the Lord imputeth not iniquity, and in whose spirit there is no guile" (vv. 1-2).

Psalm 51 was written over three thousand years ago. But it is as up-to-date as yesterday's notes from a psychiatrist's counseling session. Among other teachings, it presents to us the five steps to forgiveness.

If you would like to have your sins forgiven, to have peace with God and with yourself, and to be clean again, David told us how.

Boundless Provision

The first step to forgiveness is faith—you must believe in the love and the mercy of God. David prayed, "Have mercy upon me, oh God, according to thy lovingkindness: according unto the multitude of thy tender mercies blot out my transgressions" (v. 1).

David's appeal was for mercy. He was not the least bit interested in justice. Neither am I. Neither are you. The Scriptures say, "If thou, O Lord, shouldst mark iniquities, Lord, who could stand?" (Ps. 130:3, RSV). The word *mark* is a bookkeeping term. It means to enter into a ledger. If the Lord should place a mark against us in the ledger of eternity every time we sin, and we were called on to give an account of our sins, none of us could stand before God.

We are like the lady who went to a photographer to have her picture made. When she viewed the proofs, she expressed her displeasure to the photographer, saying, "These pictures don't do me justice." The photographer replied, "Lady, you don't need justice; you need mercy." That's a fact with all of us. None of us wants to be dealt with according to our sins.

David's appeal was to the nature of God. He asked for mercy, "According to thy loving kindness: according unto the multitude of thy tender mercies." David's prayer was, "Lord, don't deal with me according to what I am, but according to what You are."

Two young girls were standing on the deck of a ship early one morning. The older inquired of the younger,

"Isn't it a beautiful day? And look at the horizon—how beautiful it is!"

The younger girl looked at her with a bit of puzzlement on her face and asked, "What is a horizon?"

The older girl pointed off into the distance and explained, "See there where the sea rises up to the sky, and where the sky drops down to touch the sea? That's a horizon. And when you get there, it will not be there anymore. It will be gone, and there will be another and another and another, because the horizon is always farther on."

God's love and mercy are just like the horizon. Just about the time you think you have exhausted them, that you have reached their limits, you discover there are even more available.

The anonymous poem, "God's Love," expresses this truth.

> We can only see a little of the ocean,
>   A few miles distant from the rocky shore;
>   But out there—beyond, beyond our eyes' horizon,
>   Beyond the eyes' horizon,
> There's more—there's more.
>
>   We only see a little of God's loving—
>   A few rich treasures from His mighty store;
>   But out there—beyond, beyond our eyes' horizon,
>   Behold the eyes' horizon,
>   There's more—there's more!

The first step on the road to forgiveness is to believe in the love and mercy of God.

Finding Forgiveness

Sin Is Serious

The second step to forgiveness is honesty. You must acknowledge the seriousness of your sin. When we do something noble and kind, most of us are more than glad to accept the credit, but when we do something wrong, we often sidestep the blame. We excuse ourselves and accuse others.

But there was none of this in David. He honestly confessed his sin and took full responsibility for it.

Listen to him,

> For I acknowledge my transgressions: and my sin is ever before me. Against thee, thee only, have I sinned, and done this evil in thy sight: that thou mightest be justified when thou speakest, and be clear when thou judgest. Behold, I was shapen in inquity; and in sin did my mother conceive me (vv. 3-5).

David used three words to describe the wrong that he had done. The words are: *iniquity, transgression,* and *sin.* The word *iniquity* means "to twist or pervert" that which is good. God has given us His perfect law, but we have perverted and twisted it from His intended purpose.

The word *transgress* means to rebel deliberately against God. Have you ever walked in the woods, perhaps while hunting, and come upon a fenced area with a "No Trespassing" sign? If you had ignored the sign and climbed through the fence, you would have been a transgressor. To trespass means to cross over the limits or to ignore the "thou shalt not."

The word *sin* means "to miss the mark." It carries with it the idea of an archer who draws back his arrow and aims at a distant target, but his aim is off and the arrow falls short.

David then made three confessions about the wrong he

had done. First: "My sin is ever before me." David lived a haunted life. He would lie in bed at night thinking of his evil deeds. He would awaken in a cold sweat, dreaming of his wrongdoing.

Second, he said, "Against thee, thee only have I sinned...." "Wait a minute, David," we say, "didn't you sin against Bathsheba when you committed adultery with her? Didn't you sin against Uriah when you arranged his death? Didn't you sin against the child born out of your adulterous relationship?"

How could David then claim that he had sinned only against God? It is because every obligation to mankind has its foundation in the law of God. We cannot wrong a person without wronging God. We cannot strike a blow against humanity without striking a blow against God. Whatever we do that hurts other people is, first and foremost, a sin against God.

Third, David sang, "Behold, I was shapen in iniquity; and in sin did my mother conceive me."

David traced his actions back to an inborn evil nature. From the very moment of his conception the principle of sin was within him so he was a sinner from his innermost being. Therefore, he needed forgiveness not only for what he had done but also for what he was. David was born with a sinful nature.

We are all responsible for our own sins. Take a little child, for example. Before the child can either walk or talk, you can ask him, "Did you take your sister's toy?" He will shake his head. The child cannot talk, but he can lie. Where did he learn to lie? Who taught him to lie? It springs from his inborn sinful nature. Even at the moment of conception there was the possibility of sin lurking within him. It sounds incredible, but that is what the Bible teaches. The seed of deception is in us from the moment we are born.

Now, God does not hold the child accountable until he reaches an age of accountability. That is the age when he can distinguish the difference between right and wrong and has the ability to make his own choices. At that time God holds each person accountable for his own actions.

So, David's confession was this: "Lord, I have perverted Your law; I have willfully disobeyed Your will; I have failed to be what I ought to be, and I can't forget it. My sin is ever before me. The wrong I did was against You. And I not only *did* wrong, I *am* wrong. From my inmost being I am a sinner."

What honesty! That's the only way to do business with God.

The Scriptures declare, "If we confess our sins, he is faithful and just to forgive us our sins, and to cleanse us from all unrighteousness" (1 John 1:9). Confession is more than simply acknowledging that we are guilty of this or that. It means to agree with God concerning sin, to agree in the sense that we feel some of the agony and distress He feels over our rebellious actions. This kind of confession comes with genuine repentance. Without it there can be no forgiveness.

Ask and It Shall Be Given

The third step to forgiveness is prayer—you must ask God to forgive you. David not only longed for forgiveness; he *asked* for it. His desires were turned into prayers:

> Purge me with hyssop, and I shall be clean: wash me and I shall be whiter than snow. Make me to hear joy and gladness; that the bones which thou hast broken may re-

joice. Hide thy face from my sins, and blot out all mine iniquities (vv. 6-9).

David asked for cleansing three times. He prayed, "Purge me . . . wash me . . . blot out all mine iniquities." The word *purge* is a technical word for the priestly act of declaring a leper ceremonially clean.

The word *wash* is a laundry term which describes washing a garment. The word *blot* is of a scribal nature, meaning to wipe away or to erase. It is the Hebrew equivalent to the Greek word Peter used when he preached, "Repent ye therefore, and be converted, that your sins may be blotted out" (Acts 3:19).

The word *blot* is vivid. Ancient writing was on papyrus, and the ink used contained no acid. It did not bite into the papyrus as modern ink would; it simply lay on the top of it. To erase the writing one might take a wet sponge and simply wipe it away. In the same manner, God blots out the sin of the forgiven person.

That's what all of us need—to have our sins wiped away. We don't need to turn over a new leaf in life but to have the old leaf wiped clean. David's use of these three strong words revealed his desire for total and absolute cleansing from his sin.

Sin leaves a stain on our lives that only God can cleanse. A beautiful young college girl came to me for counseling. She said, "I'm expecting a baby, and I'm not married. I just don't know what to do. I can't go home to my parents because it would break their hearts. I feel so dirty."

I assured her that she could be clean again. God can do what no priest's pronouncement can do, what no laundry detergent can do, what no scribe's eraser can do. He can take away our sins. He can cleanse us completely.

"Though your sins be as scarlet, they shall be as white

as snow; though they be red like crimson, they shall be as wool" (Isa. 1:18).

Out of the Mire and into the Choir

The fourth step of forgiveness is repentance—you must be willing to turn from your sin and serve God. Honestly confessing his sin and asking for forgiveness, David vowed:

> Then will I teach transgressors thy way; and sinners shall be converted unto thee. Deliver me from blood guiltiness O God, thou God of my salvation: and my tongue shall sing aloud of thy righteousness. Oh Lord, open thou my lips; and my mouth shall shew forth thy praise (vv. 13-15).

A person who has been cleansed and forgiven will be grateful, and a grateful person will want to serve God and share what he has experienced with others. So David vowed that, once forgiven and cleansed, he would become a bold witness, a faithful teacher, and a choir member. In essence, he promised God, "When you take me out of the mire I will join the choir."

Give Him Your Heart

The fifth step to forgiveness is sincerity—you must be broken-hearted over your sin. This final step is the most important. It is possible to go through the motions of the first four steps and not be sincere. Without this the others are of no avail.

David knew the Lord was not interested in sacrifices or in burnt offerings. What God wants is a heart broken over sin, genuine sorrow for wrongdoing.

David, as the king, had thousands of cattle and sheep he could easily have offered unto God as a sacrifice, but God wanted his heart—not merely a gift laid on the altar.

The idea of paying for one's sins, making a sacrifice, seems to be ingrained in human nature. Dr. Hobart Mower, the famous psychiatrist, felt that one of the reasons psychotherapy is so successful, and so expensive, is that while people are going through it, they feel they are paying for their wrongdoings.

A man came to me, distressed over his marriage. He had been unfaithful to his wife, and she had discovered it. They were trying to put their marriage back together, and I was trying to help them. At the close of our initial conversation he told me he had bought his wife an expensive diamond ring for Christmas and wondered if he should give it to her. I answered him, "No, not under any circumstances. Wait until later."

If he had given his wife the ring for Christmas, she would have concluded he was trying to buy her off and that he had no idea of the hurt she was going through.

We can't buy God off, either. He forgives us only when we are genuinely sorry for our sins and repent of them. There is a tremendous difference between repentance and remorse. This can be seen in the difference between Simon Peter and Judas Iscariot. Simon Peter and Judas both blew it: Simon when he denied that he knew the Lord and Judas when he sold the Lord for thirty pieces of silver. One went out and wept bitterly; the other went out and hanged himself. Simon *turned back* in repentance; Judas *turned away* in remorse. Remorse is concerned with the consequences; repentance is concerned with the relationship. It is remorse to say, "Oh, Lord, forgive me and eliminate the consequences." It is repentance to say, "Oh, Lord, forgive me and cleanse me, regardless of the consequences. And if need be, double the consequences to cure me."

The basis for our forgiveness is Christ's substitutionary

death on the cross for our sins (Heb. 10:17; 11:12-14). He took the first step for us. He stepped down from heaven to earth, from glory to the cross, to pay for our sins. The next steps are up to us.

You are only five steps away from salvation, cleansing, and forgiveness. You know what they are. They are the steps of faith, honesty, prayer, repentance, and sincerity.

Take them now, and you can be forgiven.

9
Stand Up to Life
(Psalm 55)

Several years ago I visited with a psychiatrist friend. It was one of those rare occasions when one person lays bare his soul to another. This time the psychiatrist did the talking. He had been the campus physician for a large state university several years earlier. He had not handled the pressure of his job very well, and, as a result, began to use drugs until he became addicted to them. When the university officials and the state medical board learned of this, he was dismissed from his job, and his medical license was suspended.

He was so humiliated and ashamed that his first thought was to pack up and leave—not just the city but the state as well. He considered moving to California where he was not known and where he could start life over, but the more he reflected on this, the more he realized that was not the solution to his problem. He said, "I knew if I ran away, after that every time anybody thought of me he would say, 'Well, old Bill is probably out in California, still on the needle.' So," he continued, "I decided instead to stay right here among the people before whom I had disgraced myself and show them that I was a changed man." And that's exactly what he did.

He put his life back together, abandoned drugs, had his medical license reinstated, and returned to school for additional training to become a psychiatrist. He continued to live in that same little city among those same people, showing them he was a different man, something he could never have done had he run away.

But Bill's first inclination is the reaction most of us have to trouble, disappointments, and the heartaches of life. When hurts come, when we are embarrassed in some way, our first thought is to run away and start life all over again.

Who among us has not thought of and felt like doing precisely that?

Reasons for Running

Many factors can make us want to run away from life. Disappointment in ourselves or being ashamed of something we've done can make running appealing. When we have failed ourselves or others, we don't want to face people. It seems easier to run.

Sometimes our disappointment is in another person. Perhaps it is a trusted friend, a child, or a mate who hurts us. Sometimes it is even God.

Jonah, the renegade prophet, received a call, commanding him to preach in Nineveh, but he didn't want to do it. Jonah didn't like the Ninevites, and he was not willing to answer God's call as a missionary to them. So Jonah fled. He bought a ticket and boarded a ship for Tarshish—the opposite direction from Nineveh. He wanted to go as far away from God's call as possible. But Jonah learned what we all must learn sooner or later: we can't run far enough or fast enough to escape God. If we ascend into the heavens, He is there. If we go down to the depths of the sea, He is there. If we could mount on the wings of the morning and go to the uttermost parts of the earth,

He would also be there. We can't run out on God, and we can't run out on life.

But when the pressures and difficulties of life come, we think about it and we want to escape.

One Man's Story

That's why Psalm 55 is so relevant for us today. It is the story about a man who, as a result of a deep disappointment in life, longed to run away from life itself. There are two key verses in this psalm that serve as bookends to a drama from real life.

In verse 6 the psalmist sang, "I said, Oh that I had wings like a dove! for then would I fly away, and be at rest." The writer was troubled by life and surmised that if he could change his location it would change his situation.

The other bookend is verse 22: "Cast thy burden upon the Lord, and he shall sustain thee." Having contemplated running away from life, the psalmist then concluded that this was not the answer to his problem. There was a better alternative.

He concluded that the answer to life is not trying to run away from problems but rather to cast them on the Lord and receive grace from Him in order to stand up to life and be victorious over it.

The problem the psalmist faced was a profound disappointment in a dear and trusted friend. Feeling the sting of his criticism and the heat of his anger, he wished he could escape. It is significant that his problem was not an enemy. If that had been the case he could have handled it better, but a trusted friend was different. Our severest disappointments in life come from the people who are nearest and dearest to us—our children, our parents, our husbands or our wives, or our friends. When we are hurt by people we trust, then we are most distressed.

The man who hurt the writer of this psalm was one of his peers, a close companion, a familiar friend, one with whom he had talked often and who had even walked with him to the house of God to worship with him.

But something had happened; we don't know what it was. For some reason his friend turned on him and became critical of him. He even tried to hurt him. This so filled the psalmist with anxiety and anger that he wanted to run away. That's when he cried, "Oh that I had wings like a dove! for then I would fly away, and be at rest."

Three Ways to Run

Have you ever felt like running away from life? Sure you have! We all have. There are at least three ways people try to run away from life.

Some try to run away from life literally. They pack up and move out. They either run away or walk away from the people and the places that are troubling them. That's nothing new. That response to life is as old as Adam.

Do you remember the story of the prodigal son in Luke 15:11-32? He might have said to his father, "I've had it with you and all your rules. I want my freedom. Give me my part of the family inheritance, and I'll get out of your house and get you out of my hair forever." With great reluctance his father gave him his share of the family inheritance, and the boy walked away into the far country.

If you have rebellious children who want to run away from home, you are not the first parent to have to deal with that. If you don't understand your parents and you think you could make it better on your own, remember that you are not the first young person to feel like that. Those feelings go back at least as far as the story of the prodigal son, but that is not the best way to deal with life.

Running away or walking away seldom solves anything. But it is an option.

While some people run away from life literally, others run away chemically—through alcohol and other drugs. As one New Jersey addict explained it, "It's the only way a poor man can get out of Hoboken."

He was right, you know. Alcohol and drugs can put you in another world quickly and cheaply, but is the cost of the ticket worth it? I don't think so. Nonetheless, many people who find life, work, marriage, or school difficult take a "trip" on drugs.

Unfortunately, some people run away from life ultimately through suicide. Dr. C. Roy Angell, who for years was pastor of the First Baptist Church, Miami, Florida, told about a visit he made one day in response to an urgent telephone call. He arrived at two-story, palatial mansion with manicured grounds and a four-car garage. In one of the stalls was a Cadillac, in another was a Lincoln Continental, and in the others were two imported sports cars. The house gave every evidence of elegance, affluence, and prosperity.

When he walked inside he saw the most exquisite carpets he had ever walked on in his life. Every room was furnished with expensive antiques. He had been invited by the lady and to begin the conversation he said to her, "Any person who lives in a house like this must be delightfully happy." In answer she got up, walked over to a small table, opened the drawer, pulled out a pistol, and said, "Do you see this? You'll never know how many times a day I think about using this on myself."

Looks can be deceiving. Not every man who wears expensive suits, not every woman who buys designer clothes, not every young person who flashes a plastic smile on their face is really happy. Oftentimes underneath all that veneer there is a broken heart and a person who thinks of running away from life through suicide.

Edwin Arlington Robinson (1869-1935) wrote a poem that expresses this truth. It was called "Richard Cory," a man who seemed to "have it made." He was a splendid gentleman who had the admiration of the community. People wanted to be like Richard Cory . . . but the poem ends with "Richard Cory . . . Went home and put a bullet through his head.

Somewhere in the world over five thousand people take their lives every day. They find life unbearable. Unable to go on, unable to face the realities of life, they say, "I want out. I want to escape, I want to end it once and for all." They run into the shadowy land of death. Among teenagers, suicide is the third leading cause of death. Among college students it is the second leading cause of death. The professional group most prone to suicide is the medical profession. In fact, when a doctor dies before the age of thirty-nine, one out of four times it is a suicide. And do you know which segment of the medical profession is most prone to suicide? Psychiatrists.

Who besides God will ever know what rationalizations race through a person's mind to persuade him that suicide solves anything? Each one has a different breaking point; no two responses are alike when the sky seems to be falling. But for some reason, in a dark moment the person sees no hope and takes his own life.

I repeat: things are not always as they appear. It was Longfellow who said, "If we could read the secret history of our enemies, we would see in each person's life sorrow and suffering enough to disarm all hostility." We would not be nearly so critical, so caustic of others, if we knew the burdens they were bearing.

Many people who appear to be on top of life are in

reality being crushed by life. They are thinking about running away from it, literally, chemically, or ultimately, because it has become unbearable to them. They feel what the psalmist felt when he cried, "Oh that I had wings like a dove for then I would fly away and be at rest."

Grace and Gristle

But are these the only releases? Certainly not! Look around. Not all who find themselves "up against it" end up in a morgue or a sanitarium. There are those who, spiritually speaking, are like the description *Time* once gave boxer Rocky Marciano: "Most anybody can hit him; the difficulty is to hurt him. He hardens his body to take any punch, and that is what is so discouraging to his opponents."

The psalmist had found the better way to respond to life when he wrote, "Cast thy burden upon the Lord, and he shall sustain thee."

There is our alternative to running away from life. By God's grace we can have the gristle to stand up to life instead of giving way to it. We can cast our burden on Him, and He will sustain us.

The word "sustain" means "to strengthen," "to uphold." It is the same word used to describe how God provided for Israel during their wilderness wanderings. Nehemiah reminded us that while they traveled through the wilderness for forty years, God supplied their every need. Their clothes never wore out, and their feet were never swollen (Neh. 9:21). Think of that—walking for forty years and your feet never swelling. That's how completely God sustained Israel. The psalmist tells us that God will likewise care for us if we will cast our burden on Him.

It is also the same word used to describe how God sustained the prophet Elijah during a great drought (1 Kings

Stand Up to Life

17:8-9). The Lord sent him to the home of a widow who would feed him. When he arrived and asked her for a piece of bread, she had none. The poor woman had only a handful of meal in a barrel and a little oil in a vessel. Elijah told her not to be afraid to use the meal and oil she had, for God had promised to take care of her; therefore her supply would not be depleted. Elijah stayed and ate with her many days. Miraculously, neither her meal barrel nor her oil supply was depleted.

Just as God sustained Elijah, the widow, and her son, so He will sustain us if we cast our burden on Him. Somehow, in some way, He will keep us on our feet. By the same miraculous power He will give us the inner resources necessary to stand up to, and be victorious over, life.

The Lord did not promise to save us from the burdens or the blows of life but to *sustain* us in them and against them. Jesus prayed in the Garden of Gethsemane that the cup might pass from Him. It did not; He drank it. But God sustained Him in the Garden and on the cross and brought Him out of the tomb victoriously. What God did then, He can do again. He can bring triumph out of tragedy, victory out of defeat, and strength out of weakness.

We, too, may pray that the cup of cancer, sorrow, or an intolerable marriage will pass from us, but it may not. But if not, God will give us strength and divine reinforcement. Phillips Brooks said, "Do not pray for tasks equal to your powers. Pray for powers equal to your tasks." We need to pray, "Oh, God, either lighten my burden or strengthen my back." Most often we will discover that God does the latter.

The Scriptures promise, "Those who trust in the Lord for help will find their strength renewed. . . . they will run and not get weary; they will walk and not grow faint" (Isa. 40:31, GNB).

I see much suffering in the course of my work. I visit people in hospitals, console those who are bereaved, and listen to others pour out their fears and frustrations about ailing parents, wayward children, failing marriages, dead-end jobs, and the potentially serious malfunctioning of their bodies. After sharing so much sorrow, how can I still believe in the goodness of God and His world?

The answer lies in the promise of this verse. I have seen people reach the limits of their endurance and drain themselves dry of compassion, loyalty, and patience because life had asked so much from them. Then, from a source somewhere beyond themselves, they gained a sudden infusion of new strength and new hope, so that they could "run, and not get weary; . . . walk and not grow faint."

I've seen people pass through seasons of renewal in their lives. For a time they were spiritually dead, lifeless. Then, after awhile, they grew warm and revived. God, who gives new life to the earth in the springtime, sends the miracle of renewed life to His children as well.

I constantly see "ordinary" people do the most extraordinary things. I've seen them exhibit strength they had told me they didn't possess.

This morning a man visited me. One week ago he had buried his wife of over fifty years. He confessed, "I've just gone through what I had thought I could never bear, and, with God's help, it has been surprisingly easy."

How Do You Do It?

Practically speaking, how do we put this truth into practice? How do we cast our burden on the Lord?

We do it through frequent and fervent prayer. Listen

to the psalmist's words, "As for me, I will call upon God; and the Lord shall save me. Evening, and morning, and at noon, will I pray and cry aloud: and he shall hear my voice" (vv. 16-17).

It is as simple as this: when the pressures of life bear down on us, we can go to the Lord and pray, "Lord, I can't handle this. Lord, help me." And He does.

But it will not be long until we are again weighted down by our burdens. In a sense we will have taken our burden back from the Lord. What do we do then? We return to the Lord in prayer. We lay our burdens before the Lord once more. We do that morning, noon, and night, if necessary.

This is our alternative to running away from life. We can stand up to it and be victorious over it. Whether we are facing physical, spiritual, or emotional burdens, we can have inner strength to sustain us. And isn't that what we really need—inner braces for the outer pressures of life?

So, if you are burdened, pray. If you are sick, pray. If you are worried, pray. If you are afraid, pray. If you are disappointed, pray. Pray frequently and fervently. Pray! Through prayer God will sustain you. Regardless of what your burden is, take it to God through prayer.

10
Inner Space
(Psalm 66)

A commencement speaker at Yale once told the graduates, "In 1776 you conquered your fathers. In 1865 you conquered your brothers. Now, you must conquer yourselves if you are to survive and thrive."

The conquest of self is perhaps the heaviest challenge we face. We often hear about outer space, its exploration and eventual habitation. But God is far more concerned about inner space than He is about outer space.

Samuel, God's prophet, was about to anoint the wrong man as king of Israel. Listen in as God speaks to him about this, "Look not on his countenance, or on the height of his stature; because I have refused him: for the Lord seeth not as man seeth; for man looketh on the outward appearance, but the Lord looketh on the heart" (1 Sam. 16:7). Ever and always that is the emphasis of the Bible. God looks on the inside—at inner space, at our hearts—to see if they are right with Him.

This is the emphasis of the psalmist: "If I regard iniquity in my heart, the Lord will not hear me" (Ps. 66:18). The root word of "iniquity" literally means "to pervert." It is the idea of twisting a thing from its original purpose. It is one of several words in the Bible used to describe sin.

The word *regard* means "to see." It carries with it the idea of seeing something wrong in my life and being content for it to stay there. When I look into my heart and see sin, instead of confessing it and forsaking it, I may be content for it to stay there. I can enjoy it, nurse it, and cherish it. If I do that, as the psalmist says, "The Lord will not hear me."

We must learn to deal with the iniquity of inner space, with our own heart, with our own sinfulness, if we are going to have a vital relationship with God.

There is in this passage a statement about the seat of iniquity, the seriousness of iniquity, and the solution to iniquity.

The Heart of Our Problem

We have seen an apple with a wormhole. Where did the worm start? Did it start outside and work its way in, or inside and work its way out? Fruit specialists tell us that the egg was laid on the blossom, and it hatched in the heart of the apple. So, it began inside and worked its way out.

Sin is like that. The Bible repeatedly teaches us this truth. Jesus in Matthew 12:34 says, "Out of the abundance of the heart the mouth speaketh." And Matthew 15:19, He says, "For out of the heart proceed evil thoughts, murders, adulteries, fornications, thefts, false witnesses, blasphemies." That is why God is concerned with the heart.

In Scripture the word *heart* does not refer to a bodily organ, the muscle that pumps blood throughout our body but to the control room of a person's life. It alludes to the place where we make decisions—to our mind, to our will.

The Bible teaches us that the heart of human problems is the heart. If we ever see our hearts as the *heart* of our problem, then we can deal realistically with our sins.

Jeremiah wrote, "The heart is deceitful above all things, and desperately [incurably] wicked" (Jer. 17:9). The writer of the Book of Proverbs said, "[Guard your] heart, for out of it are the issues of life" (Prov. 4:23).

And James said,

> Let no man say when he is tempted, I am tempted of God: for God cannot be tempted with evil, neither tempteth he any man: But every man is tempted, when he is drawn away of his own lust, and enticed (Jas. 1:13-14).

The word *entice* is a fishing term. When you fish, you don't drop a bare hook into the water. You must provide a bait that entices a fish. Sometimes it is a colorful plastic worm. Another time it is a live, wiggling minnow. At other times it is a tasty shrimp. Then you drop it into the water and keep it dancing, jiggling up and down to attract the attention of the fish. Hopefully, the fish will pass nearby and will be unable to resist the bait. He grabs it and is hooked before he knows it.

Temptation always follows that same overall process. Notice how it works:

- Step 1: The bait is dropped.
- Step 2: The inner desire is attracted to the bait.
- Step 3: We bite the bait; we yield to the temptation, and we sin.
- Step 4: We end up hooked and cooked. That's the tragic consequence of sin.

Satan appeals to the inner desire. Without that he would have little chance of leading us into sin.

The thrust of temptation is always the same: the one who is below us (Satan) appeals to that which is within us (our desire) to draw us from the One who is above us (God.)

There is nothing outside ourselves strong enough—not even Satan—to make us sin without our consent. Sin occurs when we agree to the temptation and follow it. Satan can entice, but no person sins against his own will.

Then, that means we cannot blame our problems on our friends, on our parents, on television, on society, or on the times. We are responsible ourselves. The switch is on the inside.

If one is going to be right with God, he must be concerned about inner space, to make sure that his heart is right with God. For, "If I regard iniquity in my heart, the Lord will not hear me."

The Secret to Effective Praying

Next, the psalmist wrote of the seriousness of iniquity. "If I regard iniquity in my heart, the Lord will not hear me."

Consider for a moment the importance of prayer. It is the most vital of all Christian exercises and experiences. Without prayer you cannot have a spiritual life. You can have a religious life and a church life without prayer, but you cannot have a personal relationship with God without prayer. It is as simple as this: either we connect with God in prayer, or we do not connect with God at all. We cannot maintain a relationship with people to whom we do not talk.

This means that the rankest form of humanism is prayerlessness. When a person chooses not to pray, he is choosing to go it on his own, by his own human resources. He is saying, "I can get along without God in my life."

If prayer is so important, what then is the key to effective praying? It is not your posture in prayer. King Hezekiah prayed with his face turned to the wall, and God extended his life fifteen years (2 Kings 20:1-6). Elijah, the prophet, sat down on the ground, put his face between his knees, and prayed for rain. And it rained for the first time in three and a half years (1 Kings 18:42). Jesus prayed lying on His face (Mark 14:35). The Pharisee and the publican prayed standing up. Daniel prayed on his knees.

The posture really doesn't matter. You may pray sitting, lying, kneeling, or standing (or even hanging upside down!). And the position of your hands is of equal unimportance. Your hands may be lifted heavenward, folded in front of you, or outstretched on a cross, as were Jesus' when He died. None of these outward matters affect the effectiveness of prayer.

While no posture in prayer is taught in the Bible, the one mentioned most often is kneeling. Daniel "kneeled upon his knees three times a day, and prayed, and gave thanks before his God" (Dan. 6:10). The psalmist sang, "Come, let us worship and bow down: let us kneel before the Lord our maker" (Ps. 95:6).

Jesus withdrew Himself about a stone's throw from the rest of His disciples and "kneeled down, and prayed" (Luke 22:41). And Stephen, when he was about to be stoned, "kneeled down, and cried with a loud voice, Lord, lay not this sin to their charge" (Acts 7:60). Before Peter raised Dorcas from the dead he "kneeled down, and prayed" (Acts 9:40).

When the apostle Paul met the Ephesian elders by the seacoast he "kneeled down, and prayed with them all" (Acts 20:36). Later he wrote to these friends at Ephesus, "For this cause I bow my knees unto the Father of our Lord Jesus Christ" (Eph. 3:14). And to the Philippians he wrote that ultimately all people shall assume that posture before the Lord, for

> every knee [shall] bow, of things in heaven, and things in earth, and things under the earth; And that every tongue

should confess that Jesus Christ is Lord, to the glory of God the Father (Phil. 2:10-11).

So, if you want to emphasize a particular posture in prayer, the one mentioned most often in Scripture is kneeling. But the effectiveness of your prayer life does not depend on your knees or on your hands. *It depends on your heart.* If your heart is not right with God, God will not hear you.

The key to effective praying is not in the words you use. Since man began praying, he has tried to impress God with his lengthy and eloquent prayers, but God is not impressed. To the contrary, He is repulsed. That's why Jesus warned us about "vain repetition." There are people who make much of using "catch phrases" in prayer as though that gives them some special power. To be around them almost makes me feel as though I must be unspiritual. The muttering of meaningless words is not only useless, it is sinful. Jesus warned us not to pray like that.

When another person is praying in public, if you want to pray with them, then pray quietly enough that you do not distrub others around you. If you want to join in their prayer and affirm what they are saying, do what the Bible enjoins and say "Amen."

The word *amen* is a word of affirmation. It means "so be it" or "Lord, let it be." This is the biblical word we are to use for the affirmation of singing, preaching, and praying with which we agree (1 Cor. 14:13-16).

The key to effective praying is not in your knees, not in your hands, not in your lips. It is far deeper than that. It is in the heart.

John Bunyan testified, "In prayer it is better to have a heart without words than words without a heart." James Montgomery reminded us, "Prayer is the soul's sincere desire, uttered or unexpressed; The motion of a hidden fire that trembles in the breast. . . . Prayer is the Christian's vital breath, the Christian's native air."

To pray, we don't have to get on our knees, close our eyes, bow our heads, or even open our mouths. We can pray anywhere, anytime, about anything. There is no law that can keep any person from praying—in school or elsewhere.

Faith is not even the key to effective praying.

Do you doubt this? Read Acts 12, and you will see what I am talking about. Peter was locked up in jail. The church started praying for him, so the Lord sent an angel to unlock the jail and set Peter free. When the angel arrived, Peter was asleep. He thought it was all a dream. He couldn't believe it. He obviously had accepted his fate and was not expecting what was about to happen. The angel brought him to the house of Mary where the church was at that very moment praying for his release.

When a young lady, Rhoda, heard his voice and recognized Peter, she ran to tell the others. But they didn't believe her. They thought she had seen an angel. She kept insisting until they went to see for themselves that it was Peter. And when they saw him they were "astonished" (v. 16).

Obviously, they were not expecting an answer. It seems they were praying without really believing God was going to do anything. They had enough faith to pray but not enough to leave the door unlocked.

We can have enough faith at times to pray without having enough faith to believe our prayer is going to be answered, but that does not limit God. If God is ready to act, He can do it with or without our faith.

What, then, is the key to effective praying? It is the heart. Until your heart is right, you might as well quit praying. Everything else you do will be an exercise in futility because God will not respond to people whose hearts are not right with Him.

The Lord once advised Joshua, "[Quit praying and] Sanctify yourselves" (Josh. 7:13). Israel had sinned against God and, as a result, they were defeated by the enemy at Ai. Joshua, their leader, fell on his face before God and started asking God why He had allowed all of this to happen. That's when the Lord told him to quit praying and to sanctify himself. Sometimes we need to quit asking and start confessing. We first need to clean up our lives, and then get back to praying. Until our heart is right, nothing else will be right.

Why, then, is sin so serious? Because it separates us from God at our most vital point. It shuts us off from effective praying. Isaiah preached,

> Behold, the Lord's hand is not shortened, that it cannot save; neither his ear heavy, that it cannot hear: But your iniquities have separated between you and your God and your sins have hid his face from you, so that he will not hear (Isa. 59:1-2).

Isaiah was clear. The problem is not with the hand of God or the hearing of God but with the heart of man. James concurs: "The effectual fervent prayer of a righteous man availeth much" (Jas. 5:16). From the very beginning sin separated mankind from God. It happened in the Garden of Eden when Adam and Eve sinned. They became aware of their sin, their rebellious nature, and felt guilty. So, they began to avoid God.

They even hid from Him. The Lord called to them, and when He found them He asked, "Adam, why are you running? Adam, why are you hiding? Adam, why are you looking back? Adam, why, why, why are you A.W.O.L.—absent without leave? Why?"

Because sin divides. Sin divided in Genesis 3:8, and it has been dividing ever since.

The psalmist agreed: "If I regard iniquity in my heart, the Lord will not hear me."

The Solution to the Pollution

The third truth this verse teaches us is the solution to our sin. What is it? If I recognize sin in my heart, I do not have to let it stay there. I can repent of it. God can make me right with Him so He will hear me.

The very construction of this verse suggests that. Notice the word *if*. We have an option. *If* we see iniquity in our life, we can do something about it. The choice is ours.

How do we deal with the sin in our heart? There are three ways.

First, we must acknowledge our sin. "If we confess our sins, he is faithful and just to forgive us our sins, and to cleanse us of all unrighteousness" (1 John 1:9).

Have you watched a basketball game lately? If so, you may have noticed that at certain levels of competition, when a player commits a foul and the referee blows his whistle, that player is supposed to raise his hand. When he does, he is confessing the referee made the right call. He concurs with the referee's decision. He is saying, "I'm the guilty one. I did it. I committed the foul. Enter a mark in the record book against me."

This is the meaning of confession in the New Testament. When the Holy Spirit "blows the whistle" on us, we are supposed to admit, "Lord, I did it. I am the guilty one. I have sinned against You."

Without confessing, there can be no cleansing. We must accept full responsibility for our sins. The ability to avoid blame is frightening. It began in the Garden, but it must end with us if we are to be forgiven.

The second step is: we must forsake our sin. The Book of Proverbs says, "He that covereth his sins shall not prosper: but whoso confesseth and forsaketh them shall have mercy" (Prov. 28:13). I must first own my sin and then disown it; I must admit it and then quit it. The trouble with many people is they want God to forgive their sins without their forsaking them. That cannot be.

The third step is to make restitution whenever possible. This is the "Zaccheus Principle" (Luke 19:8). If you stole something, we need to return it. If you lied, you need to tell the truth. If you gossiped, you need to correct the story. If you have been judgmental or critical of another, you need to apologize. Whenever and wherever it is possible and profitable, you need to make restitution for your sins just like Zaccheus did (Luke 19:1-11). And I include myself!

There are times, of course, when that is impossible. If one has killed someone, that life can't be restored. If there has been an abortion, that baby can't be brought back. Some wrongs can never be undone. In those cases all we can do is confess to God and turn from our sins, but one marvelous fact about God's grace is: it is sufficient even for those situations we can do nothing about. Even if we can't undo a sin, God can forgive it and cleanse us.

God does answer prayer. This whole psalm is a song of praise to God for the fact that the Lord had heard the psalmist and had answered his prayer.

He will likewise answer your prayer. Even if you feel your prayers aren't going above the ceiling, God can come below the ceiling. His hearing doesn't depend on our hearing. He will hear you if you will deal with inner space and let Him make your heart right.

When Jesus died on the cross, His sacrifice was complete. He died to pay in full for our sins. His blood was shed for the sins of the whole world—including yours. He is the solution to our pollution. If you will commit your life to Him, He will forgive you and cleanse you. He is waiting for you to make the next move.

11
The Best Argument for Christianity
(Psalm 69:6)

A popular song of the 1920s was called "Me and My Shadow." This points to an undeniable fact: No one can escape his shadow.

A truth of far deeper significance that applies to all people, but particularly to Christians, is that each of us casts a shadow of influence on other lives, either for good or for evil.

Our Lord Himself uttered a warning about the impact of influence:

> Temptations to sin are sure; but woe to him by whom they come! It would be better for him if a millstone were hung around his neck and he were cast into the sea, than that he should cause one of these little ones to sin (Luke 17:1-2, RSV).

Christians can be woefully careless in this matter of example and, by their carelessness, contribute to the downfall of others.

This was the concern of the psalmist when he prayed,

> Let not them that wait on [hope, look to] thee, O Lord God of hosts, be ashamed [disappointed] for my sake: let not those that seek thee be confounded [embarrassed] for my sake [because of me], O God of Israel (Ps. 69:6).

This entire psalm is a prayer for deliverance offered by a man suffering for his convictions. The psalmist faced undeserved persecution because of his devotion to God. Like Jeremiah and the apostle Paul, and certainly our Lord, he faced unfounded hostility and unjust accusations. We are not sure what he had done, but in verse 9, he wrote, "For the zeal of thine house hath eaten me up; and the reproaches of them that reproached thee are fallen upon me." This may suggest that he sparked anger for trying to reform some evil practices in the Temple. This experience was later quoted about Jesus as He cleansed the Temple.

The psalmist began with a prayer—a direct and urgent plea for deliverance. He pictured himself in a life-threatening situation. He saw himself as a drowning man up to his neck in water. Part of his problem was that God seemed to neglect his cry. He had called out to God until his throat was dry and hoarse. He had cried until the tears came no more. Yet God had not answered him. Facing affliction is hard under any circumstances. It is even worse when God seems so far away from us. The psalmist had grown weary from the tension of waiting for God to hear his prayer (v. 3). His enemies who had falsely accused him were more numerous than the hairs on his head. Obviously they had accused him of stealing something and wanted it returned. He responded by restoration, even though he had not taken it (v. 4).

The psalmist made no claim at being sinless or completely innocent. He admitted his sin and knew that God knew it, but he did not deserve what was happening to him. So, in bitterness, he cried out to God.

Suddenly, he seemed to realize that even his self-pity was detrimental to the work of God. Although he had not done anything worthy of suffering as he was suffering, still his attitude was not good. Then he prayed, "Oh Lord God of the armies of heaven, don't let me be a stumbling block to those who trust in you" (v. 6, TLB).

The prayer of this psalmist that he not be a poor example, a bad influence, ought to be the prayer of God's people. Our prayer ought to encompass three areas of life: our actions, our appearances, and our attitudes.

Watch Out; They Are Watching

It is sobering to remember that God holds you accountable for your actions and your influence. So, watch out because people are watching you. Recently, I had lunch with a businessman who related a story that illustrates this truth. A few weeks before he had gone with a group of Christian men on a fishing trip to Mexico. These men make the trip every year and combine good fishing with Christian fellowship and Bible study. He was the only man on the trip who had beer in his ice chest and smoked occasionally.

One day while fishing he was smoking a cigarette and drinking a can of beer when his Mexican guide asked in broken English, "You no Christian?"

My friend replied, "Sure, I am. Why would you ask that?"

The guide pointed to the cigarette in his mouth and the beer can in his hand and replied, "Because you are smoking and drinking."

I'm not suggesting that you can't be a Christian if you smoke and drink. However, alcohol is the greatest drug problem we face in America today, and cigarettes are a major health hazard. Therefore, for the sake of your own personal well-being, and because of your influence for Christ, I recommend that you abstain from both. The fact is, other people are watching us, and sometimes they expect more out of us than we expect out of ourselves.

Sometime ago another businessman and I chatted. He had been a member of another denomination and had recently joined our church. In the other church he had been very active. Among other things he was the coach of their softball team. One day he was returning the softball equipment to the church. The parsonage was next door to the church, and his pastor was in his front yard mowing grass when he drove up. The pastor called out to him, "Hey, John, come on over when you get through, and let's have a cold beer."

John told me, "I said to myself, *I'm getting out of this church right now. Somebody in this world has got to be good.*"

People outside the church expect a lot more out of us than we sometimes realize, and we must not let them down. Somebody does have to be "good," and you and I as the people of God have been nominated. We are to be the salt of the earth and the light of the world. We are to live so people will see our good works and glorify our Father in heaven.

For the sake of our influence we must also be concerned about the appearance of things, that is, how things look.

Not all issues are absolute black and white. There are many gray areas in life. How do we live in those gray areas? There are some things entirely harmless to us and thoroughly enjoyable, but if those things are spiritually detrimental to someone else, we should not do them. The Christian should always put the well-being of others above his own wishes and desires.

The apostle Paul's advice is, "Abstain from all appearance of evil" (1 Thess. 5:22). This simply means that if there is a question, or even a suggestion of evil, about a thing, avoid it for the sake of others.

The believers in Corinth were struggling with the pagan rite that involved placing food before idols. This food was then sometimes sold in the market, and a controversy arose as to whether Christians should buy or eat such meat. Sometimes their friends who were still pagans would have a feast and serve such meat. The Christians wondered whether they should even be seen at such places participating in such activities.

The apostle Paul told them that eating meat had no personal spiritual significance one way or the other, but that the effect of a careless attitude could be disastrous for a weak Christian. He concluded, "Therefore, if food is a cause of my brother's falling, I will never eat meat, lest I cause my brother to fall" (1 Cor. 8:13, RSV).

Not many today are willing to assume Paul's position. I fear that many of us, convinced of our own freedom and of the rightness of our behavior within that freedom, forget that "None of us lives to himself, and none of us dies to himself" (Rom. 14:7, RSV). We live in the presence of God who sees and knows all. We also have about us a host of persons—some of whom we may not even know—who perhaps look to us to set an example.

Paul spoke of this in forceful terms:

> Let us no more pass judgment on one another, but rather decide never to put a stumbling block or a hindrance in the way of a brother. Do not let what you eat cause the ruin of one for whom Christ died. Do not, for the sake of food, destroy the work of God (Rom. 14:13, 15, 20, RSV).

When we go deep in our commitment to Christ, we understand that we must think not only of ourselves but also of others. We must move from the superficial to the sacrificial.

Many Christians are superficial. We put on our Sunday clothes and our Sunday smiles and talk about how we love one another. But do we love one another enough to sacrifice our own rights and privileges for the well-being of another person? This is the law of love in action. It declares, "I love you more than I love myself. I love you enough to forego something that I would like to do and that would be harmless for me. I will deny myself for you."

Keep a Good Attitude

We not only ought to be careful about our actions and our appearances but also careful about our attitudes. That may have been the thrust of the psalmist's prayer. He was experiencing unjust and undeserved persecution and was not taking it too well. He had been bitterly complaining to God about his treatment when he suddenly realized that his complaints were not a good example, either.

By our attitudes we sometimes become worse than other people are in their actions. If you are sullen and grouchy, bitter and carping, complaining and negative, you are not a good recommendation for the Lord.

Norman Vincent Peale wrote, "Some years ago en route by train from Chicago to New York I learned something that has stayed with me. I went to the dining car and was seated opposite a man and his wife. The woman was conspicuously well dressed. She was stylishly gowned, had a kingly beautiful fur piece around her shoulder, and was wearing very handsome jewelry. You didn't need unusual discernment to perceive that there must be money in the family.

"This woman was not pleased with anything. She com-

The Best Argument for Christianity

plained about the air conditioning not being adjusted properly. She complained that the tablecloth looked messy and insisted on the stewards putting on a new one. She complained about the food. She complained about the weather. Everything was wrong.

"Her husband seemed to be an easygoing, genial sort of man. He didn't seem to be paying attention to his wife's fussing. He and I got to talking. He asked what line of business I was in. I told him I was a minister. I asked what he was and he told me. Then he said, 'My wife is in business, too.'

" 'She is?' I responded in some surprise. 'I didn't take her for a businesswoman.'

" 'Oh, yes,' he said. 'She's in the manufacturing business.'

" 'Is that so? What does she manufacture?'

" 'She manufactures unhappiness. Her own unhappiness.' "

There are plenty of people who manufacture unhappiness by their bad attitudes. Such people are never a recommendation for the Lord.

In Del Rio, Texas, last fall I met a beautiful, elderly Christian lady named Mert who told me, "I grew up with a group of morbid Christians, and for years it kept me from being one. I didn't want to be like them." Who does? If you can't have joy and enthusiasm in your heart, then you will be a poor advertisement for the Lord. You will be setting a dreadful example by your attitude as much as some people do by their actions.

C. S. Lewis spoke of this: "The best argument for Christianity is Christians—their joy, their certainty, their completeness. But the strongest argument against Christianity is also Christians—when they are somber and joyless, when they are self-righteous and smug in complacent consecration, when they are narrow and repressive, then Christianity dies a thousands deaths."

I sometimes feel like the city dumping grounds. People come with all their bitterness, complaints, and negative attitudes. Christians should not be bitter, complaining, and negative. Pray that the Lord will never let you be a stumbling block or a poor example because of a bad attitude.

For us to set some sort of example is as inevitable as for light to produce a shadow. A good example is a reflection of the indwelling Christ. A good example glorifies Christ; a bad one disgraces Him.

Furthermore, the Christian's example has both a positive and a negative aspect, producing by what we do and by what we do not do, by what we say and by what we refrain from saying.

Sinful acts can "cause the enemies of God to blaspheme," as David's adultery did. How tragic when those who bear the title "Christian" are guilty of demeaning Christ's name and hindering His cause. A Christian's outward behavior should reflect the sources beyond himself and the standards pleasing to God rather than the world.

No man ever set a more consistent example of righteousness than the prophet Daniel. When a plot was hatched to discredit him with the king, his enemies mused, "We shall not find any ground for complaint against this Daniel unless we find it in connection with the law of his God" (Dan. 6:5, RSV). Then, when it was decreed that for thirty days no petition (prayer) was to be made to anyone other than the king. Daniel went to his house and "prayed and gave thanks before his God, as he had done previously" (Dan. 6:10b, RSV).

This he did three times a day before an open window, knowing his enemies would see and accuse him. What an example to all who would be faithful to the heavenly vision, regardless of the apparent consequences!

Only as Christ lives in us can we be a good influence. The shadow of our example upon those around us affects them for good or ill as they are touched by it.

For good or for ill? That is the question.

12
The Contagion of Enthusiasm
(Psalm 69:9)

"Nothing great," Ralph Waldo Emerson said, "was ever achieved without enthusiasm." That's just as true in the church as it is out of it, but some people don't seem to understand that. They know you must have enthusiasm in sports, in business, and in politics, But the church, they think, is different. So they go to a ball game and bellow like a bull, and they come to church and sit like a mute turtle. There are many church services that begin at eleven o'clock sharp and end at twelve o'clock dull!

In fact, when I attend some worship services I feel like the little boy who went to "big" church for the first time. The church had one of those memorial plaques on the wall placed there in memory of the young men from that congregation who had given their lives in the service of their country. The little boy was fascinated by the plaque. About halfway through the service he leaned over and asked, "Mother, what's that for?"

She explained, "Son, that was placed there in memory of the young men who died in the service."

The boy replied, "Which service did they die in, the morning service or the evening service?"

I have been in some services that were so dull and dead that a person could have passed away during them, and no one would have known the difference until church was over.

But that is not God's intention. The church of Jesus Christ ought to be the goingest operation in town. It ought to be the most alive, dynamic, and exciting place there is. Where it isn't, there is clearly something wrong.

The psalmist expressed how we ought to feel abut God and His work when he sang, "For the zeal of thine house hath eaten me up" (Ps. 69:9, KJV). The word *zeal* means enthusiasm. The word *eaten* means to consume, to devour, to burn hot within. So the psalmist confessed he had a burning zeal for God and His work.

When Jesus cleansed the Temple, His disciples applied this verse to Him. They remembered that the Scriptures declared that the zeal of God would "consume" the Messiah (John 2:17). Not only was David enthusiastic about God and His work, so was Jesus.

Now, what the psalmist spoke about himself and what the apostles said about Jesus also ought to be true about us. We need to have a burning enthusiasm for God and His work.

What is enthusiasm? It is not that rah-rah spirit that goes around yelling "Hallelujah" and "Praise the Lord" all the time, although that is preferable to the dullness and deadness I find in many Christians and their churches. Enthusiasm is a combination of excitement, energy, and expectancy.

The word *enthusiasm* actually comes from two words meaning "God in us." When God comes to live in us, it always results in excitement, expectancy, and energy.

Enthusiasm is often the difference between success and failure in the work of God. If we want God's work to go forward mightily, then we must be enthusiastic about it.

There are at least six facts about God's work that ought

to excite us. We ought to be excited about the meetings, the members, the ministers, the message, the mission, and the Master of the church.

It's Necessary to Survival

First, we ought to be enthusiastic about the meetings of the church. If there is anything our denomination has plenty of, it is meetings. Will Rogers was right when he quipped, "The government taxes people to build roads, and the Baptists wear them out going to meetings."

I go to so many meetings I often feel like the dying man who had been active in church all his life. A friend, seeking to comfort him, said, "Just think, Joe, in heaven there will be no partings." Joe responded, "It's not the partings I'm concerned about; I hope there will be no meetings!"

Have you heard the poem about Mary and her lamb?

> Mary had a little lamb,
> And it was quite a sheep.
> It went to all the Baptist meetings,
> And died from lack of sleep.

Meetings are important. The disciples were meeting when Jesus instituted the Lord's Supper. The church was meeting when Jesus commissioned them to be His witnesses in Jerusalem, Judea, Samaria, and unto the uttermost parts of the earth (see Acts 1:8). The church was in a prayer meeting when the Holy Spirit came at Pentecost. We are commanded as believers not to forsake meeting together until Jesus comes again (see Heb. 10:25).

Dr. Robert Gehring, a practicing physician and professor at Baylor University Medical School in Dallas, Texas, recently gave his testimony in our church. He is an ex-alcoholic and drug addict who was saved from suicide and then converted to Christ through the witness of a Christian physican. Closing his testimony he spoke of the importance of church attendance in his own life. He said, "We've got to meet together in here [in the church] if we are going to survive out there [in the world]."

We don't go to church to score points with God. There will be no perfect-attendance awards in heaven. We should go to church for the blessings we receive and share with our brothers and sisters in Christ. We go to meet God, to make friends, to find inspiration to keep going, and to grow in Christ.

We must never have meetings merely for their own sake. They must be worthwhile and important. If we are going to take time for them, then we need to see to it that they are interesting and alive. We need to put our best into them and be enthusiastic about them.

We Are the Church

Second, we ought to be enthusiastic about the members of the church. Strictly speaking, people aren't "in" the church, they "are" the church. Buildings aren't the church; people are. Not until the third century AD did Christians begin to build buildings in which to meet.

Paul expressed this truth when he spoke of the church as the "house of God" (1 Tim. 3:15). The word *house* means "household" or "family." The church is the family of God. God is our Father, and that makes all believers brothers and sisters in Christ.

To understand this concept of the church will tremendously affect almost all we do as a church. This concept of the church largely explains much of what we do before, during, and after worship at the church I serve as pastor.

It explains why we do as we do before our services. If you came to our church before worship you might feel we are irreverent. It is like a beehive with people laughing, talking, and visiting with one another.

That troubles some people. They believe that when you go to church you ought to sit quietly in meditation prior to worship. Frankly, I have never seen any logic in getting over two thousand people together to sit and be quiet. If you want to sit and be quiet, stay at home by yourself. When the church comes together, it should be more like a family reunion. People should enjoy one another, visit with and talk to one another.

This concept also explains why we do what we do during our worship services. Our worship services are relaxed and informal. If the church is a family, then there is no need for the minister to try to impress people with how dignified, holy, or smart he is. He simply needs to tell them what the Heavenly Father says in a plain and clear manner. If the church is a family, then the worship service ought to be warm and relaxed.

One's family should be one of the few gatherings where one can relax and be himself. The church, to some degree, ought to be like that. I tell people all of the time, "If I'm ever in a wreck on my way home, people will declare I'm drunk." The nearer I get to home, the more of my clothes I take off. I loosen my tie, unbutton my shirt sleeves, and untie my shoes. When I walk in the house, clothes start flying in every direction, so I can change into more casual clothes. Home is the one place where I can be comfortable and relax. While we can't go quite that far in church, it ought to be a place where we can relax and be comfortable.

The concept of the church as a family also explains why we fellowship as we do after the services. It explains why we are loving, accepting, and forgiving toward one another.

In my family we have three children. Our older boy is twenty-five, and our only daughter is twenty. For the first time in twelve years we no longer have any teenagers in our house. Hurrah! Those two boys of mine, I believe, were out to prove that everything ever said about a preacher's kids was an understatement. As far as I'm concerned, anybody who raises teenagers in today's world should have no fear of nuclear war! But, with all of our problems, they are still my children and a part of our family, so we love them, accept them, and continue to help them, even though circumstances are not ideal.

In most families, there are various levels of maturity. It is a part of a family's responsibility to help each person grow from his/her present level of maturity to his/her full potential.

We must realize that in the church, the family of God, there are also different levels of maturity. Some people are mature and well grounded in the faith. Others are spiritual adolescents. Still others have just been born again. To be a family means that we accept one another, encourage one another, and help one another to grow to the fullness of the stature of Christ.

So we must be enthusiastic about the family of God—the members of the church.

Follow the Leader

Third, we ought to be enthusiastic about the ministers of the church. There is a movement abroad today that looks with disdain upon ministers, as though they were hirelings or religious hucksters. Such a movement cannot be of God. The apostle Paul wrote that God has given gifted leaders as a part of His spiritual gifts to the church (Eph. 4:11-12). If God calls them His gifts, we cannot look upon them as "booby prizes."

We need to remember that churches rise and fall with leadership. There are no really great churches without great leaders. It is not God's will that His church be run by a committee or governed by a board. It is His will that His church be led by a loving shepherd. As a fellow minister commented to me recently, "It is the pastor's job to feed and to lead. It is the church's job to follow and to swallow."

I would hope that the pastor's leadership would not be hard to swallow. But I repeat, there are no great churches without strong leaders who are loved and honored. No church can ever be alive and thrive, go and grow, and glow where that spirit does not prevail. The great churches are those where the pastor is respected, prayed for, and followed.

One time Israel had severe problems when it elected the twelve spies to scout out the Promised Land. They returned with glowing reports, but . . . Israel was truly "a land flowing with milk and honey," but there were also "giants in the land" and walled cities. To those fainthearted spies, the giants looked bigger than God. Only Joshua and Caleb believed they could conquer the land. So the spies gave a divided report to the nation. Two said *Go* and ten said, *No*. They couldn't even agree among themselves. As a result, Israel wandered for forty years in the wilderness, and every person above twenty years of age died without seeing the Promised Land. I know of some churches that have been in the wilderness longer than that because they followed the recommendation of a committee rather than the command of God!

Israel made two mistakes. The first was to send out the spies. You don't appoint a committee to check out God. Their second mistake was to follow the committee's recommendation. Promised Lands are never taken by committee recommendations or by majority vote, but by a few people with a daring faith seeking God. To the majority, the giants always appear bigger than God.

The straightest route from Egypt to Israel is approximately two hundred miles. If the children of Israel had taken it, they could have been in the Promised Land in eleven days. Instead, they wandered over seven hundred miles of desert for forty years. That calculates at an average of twenty miles per year or one hundred yards per day! (About the average speed for most committees.) I'm not against committees, but the action of Israel does confirm what I read on a plaque:

> If something is urgent, do it yourself.
> If you have time, delegate.
> If you have forever, appoint a committee.

My friend Jim Brown used to say, "God so loved the world that He didn't send a committee."

Committees have their place, but it is to implement, not to lead. We don't need committees on evangelism; we need people committed to evangelism. We need people who love, honor, and follow their leaders.

We not only need to be enthusiastic about our leaders, we need leaders who are enthusiastic. Any preacher not fired with enthusiasm should be fired—with enthusiasm.

New Zeal for the Old Story

Fourth, we need to be enthusiastic about the message of the church. Our message is the good news. "God was in Christ, reconciling the world unto Himself. . . . we pray ye in Christ's stead, be ye reconciled to God" (2 Cor. 5:19-20).

Christ tasted death for all men. Through faith in Him

we can experience abundant life now and eternal life when we die.

Elizabeth Swank, the widow of Fred Swank, who pastored the Sagamore Hill Baptist Church of Fort Worth for over forty years, told that after their retirement they went to Holland for one year on a special assignment for their denomination's foreign mission board.

While there they often visited military cemeteries and walked among the graves, reading epitaphs. Elizabeth saw an epitaph which she will never forget. It read, "To the world just another one—to us the only one in the world." Those words had been placed there by the loving hands of a father and mother whose only son lay beneath the sod.

That's how we feel about Jesus. To the world He is just another one. To us He is the only one in the world. There is no other name given under heaven whereby persons must be saved. He is the Way, the Truth, and the Life. No one comes to the Father but by Him (see Acts 4:12; John 14:6).

The old, old story must be told with new freshness. The bread of life must not be allowed to grow stale in us. We must stay excited about the message of the church.

Our Mission—The Great Commission

Fifth, we must be enthusiastic about the mission of the church. No church needs to sit around wondering why it is here. Our mission has been set out for us, once and for all. Jesus commanded that we are to go and disciple all nations, baptizing them in the name of the Father, the Son, and the Holy Ghost: teaching them to observe all the things that He commanded us (see Matt. 28:19-20).

Our task is to evangelize, baptize, and disciple the whole world. We have called this passage "The Great

Commission," but because of our failure to carry it out we ought to call it "The Great Omission." We have committed it to memory, but not to practice.

The church is to be both obstetrician and pediatrician. The obstetrician delivers the baby. The pediatrician doctors it to maturity.

In the same manner, the church is to help people be born into the kingdom of God through faith in Christ. Once that has happened, the church must help the newborn babes grow to full Christian maturity. That is an exciting mission.

It's His Church

Sixth, we need to be enthusiastic about the Master of the church. You know who that is, don't you? Christ! He is the Head of the church (see Eph. 5:23).

Sometimes we forget that. Often when people have been members of a church for a long time, when they have had a part in erecting its buildings, they become possessive of it.

We can become like the rich man who drove a visitor around his community, showing him the sights. He pulled up in front of a church, rolled down the window of his automobile, pointed to the sanctuary, and proclaimed, "That's my church." The visitor said, "Oh, do you belong to that church?" The man replied, "No, it belongs to me."

Strictly speaking, the church is not yours! Nor is it ours! It is *His*, or it is no church at all. We must not forget that. Sometimes children think the pastor owns the church. One Friday night I received an unusual call from an eight-year-old boy. He said, "Brother Paul, I'm at the Family Life Center, and they won't give me any popcorn. Would you tell them to give me some?" That was a strange request. We sell refreshments at our recreation facility, so

I had him put the girl in charge on the phone, and I asked her to give it to him and put it on my bill. I then promptly forgot the whole matter. The next Sunday the little boy showed up at my study with a note and seventy-five cents. His mom had found out about the call and made him write me an apology and pay me for his refreshments. The note went: "Dear Paul, I am sorry I called you. Here is seventy-five cents for the popcorn. I thought you owned the church. Miles"

Some pastors and some leaders feel like Miles. They think they own the church, too. But, in reality, the church is His, and we must always seek to know and do His will.

Let's get enthusiastic about the Master of the church—His leadership, His will, and His plan. Then the church will go forward with power.

We all should heed the admonition of the apostle Paul to Timothy: "Stir up the gift of God, which is in thee" (2 Tim. 1:6). The word *stir* means to "fan again to flame." Enthusiasm and dedication to God's word had once burned brightly in Timothy's heart, but through the years the fire had gone down. He had lost his zeal, his excitement. He had neglected the fire. Now it needed his attention. If Timothy would only fan the burning coals, they would burst into flame once more.

Some of us need the same experience. Have you lost the twinkle in your eye, the spring in your step, and the song in your heart? Does the dull gray ash of complacency cover your soul?

What has happened? You yourself may not even know. Whatever it was, the fire can burn again, but you must stir it again with renewed prayer, Bible study, and service. A zeal for God's Word needs to consume us.

We live in a cold world. People are drawn to a warm fire. If the love of Christ, concern for the lost, and a dedication to the will of God burns hot within us, people will come to watch the flame.

13
Faith Amid the Fire
(Psalm 73)

If we are honest, most of us will admit there are times when we are tempted to turn away from God. That's why Psalm 73 is so timely. It speaks to us because it is the confession of a man just like us—a man whose faith grew dim.

This psalm is a leaf from the diary of a man whose faith was on trial. He had been trying to do right, but everything had gone wrong. The result was that his faith had become weak. He had become so foolish and ignorant that he had acted like a beast before God.

What honesty! That is one of the great values of the Psalms. I know of nothing in the spiritual life more discouraging than to meet a person who gives the impression that he or she is always walking on the mountain top, living in continual sunshine with perpetual blue skies, and that he or she is always perfectly happy. That was certainly not true with the people in the Bible. They knew what it was to be cast down, perplexed, discouraged. If you don't experience these emotions, then you have nothing in common with the Bible writers. They were fallible creatures who had difficult struggles with life and its problems. This writer related one such experience.

He began his story in a remarkable way—with his conclusion. It is a dynamic, triumphant note, "Truly God is good to Israel, even to such as are of a clean heart" (v. 1). It is as if he said, "Now, I am going to tell you a story; I am going to tell you what happened to me; but let me first state my proposition, my conclusion. The thing I want to leave with you is just this—God is always good to His people." That's the message of this psalm. It seems to me that if a person keeps believing that, no matter what, he will live a victorious, well-adjusted life.

The avenue by which the psalmist arrived at this conclusion is a principle that will engage us. This man had gone through an experience that had badly shaken his faith. As a result he had acted foolishly and almost turned from God. He expressed his perplexity: "But as for me, my feet were almost gone; my steps had well nigh slipped" (v. 2).

What was the cause of his trouble? Simply that he did not quite understand God's dealings with him. The first rung that led him down is found in verse 3, "When I saw the prosperity of the wicked." When he looked at the ungodly he saw them succeeding from every standpoint. They increased in wealth. They seemed to have no fear of death. They died peaceably and painlessly. They did not appear to have the troubles other people had. They were arrogant, deceitful, blasphemous. Their eyes stood out with fatness, their pride covering them like a golden necklace (see vv. 3-12).

His own life was in stark contrast to theirs. He was trying to live right. He was avoiding sin; he was meditating upon the things of God; he was spending his time in prayer; he was in the habit of examining his life, and whenever he found sin, he confessed it and forsook it. He was seeking to live a life pleasing to God. Yet, "All the day long," he wails, "have I been plagued, and chastened every morning" (v. 14).

He was undergoing difficulty. He did not tell us exactly what was happening. It may have been an illness, trouble in his family, economic reversals, or difficulty with his children. Whatever it was, it was grievous and hurtful, and he was being tried sorely. Everything seemed to be going wrong, and nothing seemed to be going right.

This was what caused the psalmist his pain and trouble. He believed God to be holy, righteous, and true, one who intervenes on behalf of His people and surrounds them with love and care. But it seemed that God hadn't done that. How could he reconcile this with what was happening to him, and with what was happening to the ungodly?

Psalm 73 is a classic statement of this particular problem—God's way with mankind, and especially God's way with His own people. That perplexed the psalmist as he contrasted his own lot with that of the wicked.

This is a very dangerous position, for he told us his faith wavered severely. He became envious of these foolish, arrogant people. They were doing well, and not troubled like other persons, and he secretly longed to be like them. He had begun to feel it was no use trying to live right and serve the Lord. He felt that he had cleansed his heart and washed his hands for nothing. He was even at the point of blaspheming God. All that restrained him was the fear that he might influence someone else to do wrong (see vv. 15-16).

Look at his apparent logic. "After all," the psalmist in effect said, "I'm living a godly life, and this is what happens to me. Those other men are blaspheming God and with lofty utterance are saying things which should never be thought, let alone said. Yet they are very prosperous, their children are doing well; they have more than their hearts could wish. Meanwhile I am suffering the exact opposite. There is only one conclusion to draw: It is useless to try to do right. It doesn't pay to serve the Lord."

Have you ever felt like that? You may be passing through this kind of experience right now. You may be having a hard time. Blow upon blow may be descending upon you. You have been living the Christian life, reading your Bible, working for God, and yet troubles have piled one on top of another. While you try to do right, everything seems to be going wrong. To make matters worse, the unrighteous seem to be "fat and sassy." You are discouraged. You are wondering if it pays to serve Jesus. You've questioned if there is any use in seeking to live right at all. You are "in the pits."

If that is your case, you need to hear, carefully and prayerfully, this man's testimony. You must walk with him through his experience and see what saved him, what kept him from falling, what brought him out on the other side praising God for always being good to His people.

What saved this psalmist? He went into the sanctuary of God. "Then understand I their end." When he went to church his thinking was straightened out. He began to see life in a different light. He did not merely feel better; he was put right in his thinking about others, about himself, and about God. He did not merely forget about his problem for the time being; he found a solution to it. Our faith should not act as a drug on us. It is not to be "the opiate of the people." It was not intended as an escape but to give us solutions to life's problems.

In fact, if our worship does not give us a better understanding of life, then there is something wrong with it, and we would be as well off without it.

There is a living lesson for us here. It is this: the absolute necessity in the Christian life of being able to think spiritually. The whole trouble with the psalmist and with us is that we often approach our problem solely in terms of our own thoughts and our own understanding. We see things only from the human standpoint, here below. We think logically and rationally instead of spiritually. We need to see things from God's point of view—from above.

Spiritual thinking is not irrational or illogical. It is thinking of life from a higher level. The difference between them is that rational thinking is on ground level only; spiritual thinking is equally rational, but it takes in a higher level as well as the lower. It takes in all the facts, not merely some of them. It sees things from God's point of view—from above.

It is especially important to think spiritually if we are to understand God's dealings with us. That was the psalmist's problem. Why does God allow these things? Why are the ungodly allowed to profit? If God is God, why doesn't He wipe them off the face of the earth? And, on the other hand, if God is God, why does He allow me to suffer as I am suffering at the present time? This is the problem—trying to understand how God operates.

Now, in the last analysis, there is only one answer. It is found in Isaiah 55:8, "For my thoughts are not your thoughts, neither are my ways your ways, saith the Lord." That is the ultimate answer. The first thing we must realize, God teaches us, is that when we come to consider Him and His ways, we must not do so on that familiar low level, because His thoughts are higher than our thoughts, and His ways are higher than our ways.

A part of the psalmist's problem was that he had been staying away from corporate worship, as we all tend to do when we fall into this kind of difficulty. He needed desperately to return to the presence of God, into spiritual things, to see things from God's point of view. That is one of the supreme values of going to church. Without spiritual thinking, we cannot make it too well in this world.

What did he come to understand when he entered the

house of God? Three truths: the fate of the wicked, the foolishness of his own ways, and the faithfulness of God.

What he saw and learned, we also need to see and learn. If we are troubled by the prosperity of the wicked and our own seemingly unjust suffering, it will save us from the same despair and faith-shaking questions he experienced.

Seeing Life to the End

The first fact he learned in church was the fate of the wicked: ". . . then understand I their end. Surely thou didst set them in slippery places: thou castedst them down into destruction" (vv. 17-18).

A part of the psalmist's problem was that he was looking only at the present. In the house of God he began to see life as a whole instead of merely in part. The truth was that the wicked were "in slippery places." In spite of appearances, their prosperity was temporary. Ultimately, they would fall and pay for their sins in judgment. He realized that he had been looking only at their prosperity, not at their punishment. His problem was that his thinking had been partial and incomplete.

I suppose, in the last analysis, one of our central troubles is that we judge too much on the moment. We do not take the long view and see things to their end.

Things are not always as they appear. That is the whole story of the Bible. Look at the world before the Flood and after. Look at Sodom and Gomorrah before and after. What a fool Abraham seems, wandering among the mountains with sheep, in contrast with Lot's prosperous situation in the cities of the plain, with their vice and immorality. We might have asked, "Does it pay to be godly?" But wait until the end. See the final chapter, and then you will know the answer to your question.

Our Lord pointed out the need of seeing life to the end in his Sermon on the Mount.

> Enter ye in at the strait gate: for wide is the gate, and broad is the way, that leadeth to destruction, and many there be which go in thereat: Because strait is the gate, and narrow is the way, which leadeth unto life and few there be that find it (Matt. 7:13-14).

Do you see what He is saying? Look at the broad way, how marvelous it seems. You can go with the crowd, you can do what everybody else is doing, and they are all smiling and joking. Wide and broad are the gates and the way. The other seems so miserable—"strait is the gate"—one at a time, personal decisions, fighting self, taking up the cross—"strait is the gate, and narrow is the way." Because they look only at the beginning, many people are on the broad way. What is the matter with them? They do not look at the end. "Wide is the gate, and broad is the way, that leadeth to destruction." "Strait is the gate, narrow is the way," but in the end it "leadeth unto life." The end of one is destruction; the other, life.

If you take your view of life from the newspaper, Hollywood, or television soap operas, you may well think that the non-Christian world is having a terrific time with its pomp, glory, and wealth. But it does not matter what the temporary prosperity of the ungodly may be. Although, at this moment, appearances may be to the contrary, it is a certain fact that those who are far from God shall perish (v. 27).

Look at the end of those people. Look at them passing in and out of the divorce courts as they turn marriage into licensed prostitution. See them addicted to alcohol and drugs. See them commit suicide, and you know something of "the end" of their ways. When people are attracted by appearances, they look only at the surface, only at the beginning. They do not look at this type of life to its end; they give no thought whatever to the ultimate outcome. Nevertheless, it is as true today as it has ever been; the Bible has always stressed that the end of these things is "destruction."

We need the insight of Moses. He is a good example of a man who took the long view in life. The result was that he chose "rather to suffer affliction with the people of God, than to enjoy the pleasure of sin for a season" (Heb. 11:25). Age and decay, death and judgment are certain. The most terrible thing about sin is that it blinds people to the realization of this. They do not see that their pomp and glory are but for a season.

The psalmist saw this so vividly in the sanctuary of God that he not only ceased to be envious of the ungodly, he began to feel sorry for them as he realized the truth about their position.

Don't Be Like an Animal

When the psalmist realized the fate of the wicked, he became embarrassed about what he had thought. He wrote of himself, "Thus my heart was grieved and I was pricked in my reins [innermost being]. So foolish was I and ignorant: I was as a beast before thee" (vv. 21-22). In church he realized his thinking had not only been faulty, it had been foolish and almost fatal. The word *foolish* means stupid. He confessed he was like a beast, utterly irrational, behaving in a stupid, absurd manner.

What is the difference between a beast and a person? I have already partly suggested the answer. Surely one of God's supreme gifts to us is understanding and reasoning —the power to think. An animal may be highly intelli-

Faith Amid the Fire

gent, but it lacks the power of reasoning, however much it may sometimes appear to the contrary.

In what respect had the psalmist been like an animal in his thinking? He had doubted God because God did not act immediately, and he had expected a trouble-free life to begin with. He had felt that because God had not acted immediately, He would not act at all. Such thinking was unfounded. He had either forgotten or never learned. As Longfellow put it:

> Though the mills of God grind slowly,
> Yet they grind exceeding small;
> Though with patience he stands waiting,
> With exactness grinds he all.

In church, he realized that God's justice would ultimately reign. And he saw himself as foolish for even questioning it. The psalmist also found he had been stupid because he had obviously entertained a false idea of the godly life. He had thought his life would be a long round of sunshine and happiness. That made him complain and moan, "I have cleansed my heart in vain and washed my hands in innocence. All day long I have been plagued and chastened every morning."

Isn't this true of all of us? We tend to accept all of the gifts, the pleasures, the happiness, and the joys of life without saying much to God about it, but the moment anything goes wrong, we begin to grumble. We take our health and strength, our food and clothing, and our loved ones for granted. But the moment anything goes wrong we start complaining, "Why should God do this to me? Why should this happen to me?"

We seem to think that, as Christians, we should never have any trouble. Nothing should ever go wrong for us; the sun should always be shining around us, while all who are not Christians, on the other hand, should undergo constant trouble and difficulty—but the Bible has never promised that. It rather promises, "that we must through much tribulation enter into the kingdom of God" (Acts 14:22). It also says, "Unto you it is given in behalf of Christ, not only to believe on him, but also to suffer for his sake" (Phil. 1:29).

God did not save Daniel from the lions' den; he saved him *in* it. God did not save the three Hebrew children from the fiery furnace; He saved them *in* it. God did not save David from the valley of the shadow of death, but He saved him *in* it. He did not route him around the valley of the shadow of death; He became his Shepherd and walked with him *through* it.

So, the psalmist discovered that he had largely been producing his own trouble and unhappiness. He found in the sanctuary of God that his trouble was not really the ungodly at all; it was himself! He had worked himself up into this condition.

Great Is Thy Faithfulness

Finally, in church he understood the faithfulness of God.

> Nevertheless I am continually with thee: thou hast holden me by my right hand. Thou shalt guide me with thy counsel, and afterward receive me to glory. Whom have I in heaven but thee? and there is none upon earth that I desire besides thee. My flesh and my heart faileth: but God is the strength of my heart, and my portion for ever (vv. 23-25).

Notice this blessed word—"nevertheless." The psalmist seemed to be saying, "I have failed; I have gone wrong; I have not done my duty. Nevertheless, I am still in God's presence. God is faithful, though I have not been. God has not blotted me out. He has allowed me to be forever in His presence."

This is truly amazing grace. He realized that though he had failed God, God had not failed him. God held him up and kept him from falling completely. He had almost slipped. Why? It was because God had a firm grip on him and held him up. God has promised to keep us from falling. He has promised that no one can snatch us out of the Father's hand. God is faithful to keep us.

Then he related three things God is faithful to do for us. First, He saves us. "Thou shalt guide me with thy counsel, and afterward receive me into glory" (v. 24). The word *receive* is a Hebrew word meaning "to take." It is used in both the experience of Enoch (Gen. 5:24) and in that of Elijah (2 Kings 2:11). In the same way that God took Enoch and Elijah into heaven, so He will also take us into His presence. The idea of heaven and eternal life are not fully revealed in the Old Testament, but we gather a glimpse of them from passages like this.

Second, God satisfies us. "Whom have I in heaven but thee? and there is none on earth that I desire beside thee" (v. 25). The psalmist came to the conviction that God was all he had and all he needed. If he had God he didn't have to have all the answers to all of life. He could trust the faithfulness of the Father.

Have you arrived at a knowledge of God and an experience with God such as the psalmist had? Can you honestly say, "Whom have I in heaven but thee? and there is none on earth that I desire beside thee"? The psalmist had reached the point where he felt God was enough. Even if there are troubles and trials in life, he had God; that was sufficient.

Third, God strengthens us. "My flesh and my heart

faileth: but God is the strength of my heart, . . . forever" (v. 26).

Then he made a commitment of himself to God. Here, in view of all of his experience, he could do nothing but give himself to the worship and adoration of God. So he made three resolutions in verse 28.

First, he resolved to keep near God. He realized that there is only one thing that matters, and that is a personal relationship to God. "If a man is near to God," said this man, "it does not really matter what happens to him. But if a man is far from God, nothing can eventually be right." This was his very profound conclusion.

Second, he resolved to trust the Lord—even when he did not understand what was happening.

Third, he resolved to share with others what God had done in his life. He would become a witness, a worker for God.

Have you come to this place of dedication? Can you say without reservation and without hesitation, that God is always good to His people?

We must be careful. We must be fair to ourselves and fair to God. This promise of God is vast and all-inclusive, but it is also conditional. It is to them who are of a clean heart. In other words, if you and I sin against God, then He will have to deal with us, and it is going to be painful. But even when God chastens us, it is still good for us, because we are His children.

I sometimes think the very essence of Christianity, and the secret of a successful spiritual life, is merely to realize the truth found in these first two verses: "Truly God is good to Israel, even to such as are of a clean heart. But as for me, my feet were almost gone; my steps had well nigh slipped." In other words, I have complete, absolute confidence in God and none in myself. That is the essence of the Christian life. Have you yet come to that place of commitment?

14
Banishing Discouragement
(Psalm 77)

Discouragement is the common cold of our emotions. Eventually it affects us all. Elijah, God's iron man of the Old Testament, became so discouraged that he sat down under a juniper tree and prayed to die. Jesus Himself often "sighed" deep within His spirit (Mark 8:12).

The apostle Paul had so many difficult experiences in Asia that he "despaired even of life" (2 Cor. 1:8). The word "despaired" means "to be at utter loss." The circumstances Paul faced seemed so hopeless he saw no way out but death.

Winston Churchill confessed that he was often hounded by the "black dog" of despair. And Charles Haddon Spurgeon, perhaps the greatest preacher since the apostle Paul, in spite of his sparkling wit and quick humor, fought continual bouts with depression as a result of gout that finally killed him at the age of fifty-eight.

If you are singing the blues in your life, it might help you to know that the psalmist understood such feelings. We read about them in Psalm 77.

The man we meet in this psalm bore all the marks of depression. He was looking at life through dark-colored glasses. He had dialed heaven's number on his prayer line and gotten a busy signal. He felt forgotten and forsaken by God.

In his search for answers to his problems he couldn't sleep, and so he counted the days of the past instead of sheep. He had aphasia. He was unable to articulate his thoughts due to emotional exhaustion. He was so tired he couldn't speak. He lived in retrospect. He remembered when he used to be happy and had a song in his heart—but no more.

He even began to question God (vv. 7-9). Questions never seem lacking at such times in our lives. "Has God rejected His people?" "Does He no longer care?" "Has He lost His compassion?" These are sharp, piercing questions.

The questions came from a heart that thought God could, but He wasn't doing what He ought to do. The psalmist was asking, "Why me, Lord?" His primary concern was the absence of any sign of God's compassion and power.

There is always a progression in such emotional experiences. Despair begins with a disappointment that is not handled constructively. The pattern is: disappointment, discouragement, doubt, depression, and despair. Disappointment that leads to doubt is therefore the father of despair.

Some of you, like the psalmist, are questioning God's divine ability to do anything with your problem right now. That's the condition the psalmist was in, the doubting stage of life. Every one of us can identify with this mood.

The psalmist then came to a saving insight. He said, "This is my infirmity" (v. 10). He recognized that the problem was with himself, not with God.

He realized that his doubts were due to his own weakness, not to God's negligence. At this point he determined to do something about his discouragement. Four times in verses 10 and 11 he says, "I will . . . ." This is significant.

We are not helpless victims of our emotions. We do not have to be hijacked by our attitudes. We can take action. Our thoughts govern our moods, therefore, if we think right, we will feel right. Most depression arises from erroneous thinking, and we have within us the power to change and to control our thoughts.

In dealing with discouragement and depression, one must be mentally tough. If you don't handle your emotions, they will handle you. You must make up your mind that you are not going to let the circumstances of life defeat you. You will defeat them. Fight! Fight! Fight! Never give in. The choice is yours. Make up your mind. Say it in your heart: *I am going to conquer this. I will not let this get the best of me.* Say it again. Say it a thousand times, if necessary. But never give up or give in.

How are we as Christians to cope with the disappointments of life? In the fourth division of this psalm (vv. 11-20) the psalmist told us what he did. As we learn what he did to overcome discouragement, we find help for ourselves. Out of his experiences we can learn three valuable truths about how to handle discouragement and disappointment in our own life.

Look in the Book

Memory is one of man's noblest assets, but it must be used with selectivity and with discipline. What the psalmist had been remembering in his sleepless and troubled nights had not helped him. These memories had, in fact, led him into deeper difficulty. Now he declared that he would remember the great deeds of the Lord and the miraculous wonders of old (vv. 11-12).

One approach will help you deal with depression is to study God's Word and recall His mighty works in other days. Remembering God's deeds in the past as they are related in Scripture, recalling what God has done in and through His people Israel, can strengthen our faith for today.

If you are discouraged, may I ask you, how much time do you spend in the Bible? Recalling the wonders of God in the past brings hope for the present.

Sometimes people remark to me, "I wish I had more faith. I wish I could increase my faith." My advice to them is to start reading the Bible. Paul said, "Faith cometh by hearing, and hearing by the word of God" (Rom. 10:17). If you want to have more faith, then dig into the Bible more.

But we must not stop at remembering God's works in the Bible. We should also recall what He has done in our own experience. All of us have a spiritual history, a biography we need to keep fresh in our minds.

Dickens, in his story "The Haunted Man," had the chemist pray, "Lord, keep my memory green." Have you so soon forgotten the time when you received the Savior and the joy, assurance, and security which came as a result of your decision? Have you so soon forgotten the deliverance God has wrought in your life?

What about the time when your child was sick; your business was almost flat; your home almost broken; you were almost in an automobile accident? And you heard a sermon exactly when you needed it, and God met all of your needs!

Don't let your memory of God's mighty deeds in the Scripture and your own life wither and fade. If you want to deal effectively with discouragement, you must go into the Book and remember God's deeds of the past.

Keep an Attitude of Gratitude

As the psalmist focused on what God had done in the past, he broke out into a song of praise. He declared, "Who is so great a God as our God? Thou art the God that doest wonders" (vv. 13-14). Out of his despair he looked not at his miserable circumstances but at God, and this uplook brightened his outlook. In his gloom he looked up and cheered up. Even in despair he kept an attitude of praise.

Keeping an attitude of gratitude can be redemptive to anyone. It helps to stop pouting and start praising.

It is easy to rejoice in times of prosperity, but we must learn to thank God when everything is "going to pot." God wants us to rejoice in Him, not in our circumstances. He is just as real in our defeats as in our victories. He is just as close in our sicknesses as He is in our health. God is just as near in times of sorrow as in times of joy.

More people rejoice in their success than in the Lord. Jesus taught the seventy who went out and met with such great success that they should "rejoice not, that the spirits are subject unto you; but rather rejoice, because your names are written in heaven" (Luke 10:20).

We must not find our joy in our success, but in our relationship. The time will come when we go out and the spirits are not subject to us. Then where will we be? We will still be in a right relationship with Him, and that's where our joy should be. We must learn to be happy *with God Himself,* not only with His gifts and benefits.

A young bride from the East Coast followed her husband to an army camp located on the edge of the Mojave Desert in California. The only housing available was a run-down shack near an Indian village. The heat was unbearable in the daytime—115 degrees in the shade! A hot wind blew all the time, and dust covered everything. The young wife's days were long and boring, and her only neighbors were Indians, none of whom spoke English. She was miserable and complained continually.

When her husband was sent off for two weeks of maneuvers, his bride became so despondent she wrote her mother that she was coming home. She couldn't take it anymore. The mother's response was a quotation from Fredrick Langbridge:

> Two men look out through the same bars:
> One sees mud, and one the stars.

The wife decided to accept the situation and look for the stars. First, she made friends with the Indians. She learned to speak their language and learned to make their crafts. She began to notice the beautiful sunrises and sunsets of the desert. Then she began to study the desert and discover its beauty. She learned about its past and its plants. She became an expert on that area and later wrote a book about it.

What had changed? Not the Indians. Not the desert. She had. By accepting the situation which had caused frustration, she transformed her circumstances.

The same thing can happen with us. Most depression arises from erroneous thinking, and we have within us the power to control these thoughts that keep us in needless gloom. An attitude of gratitude will help us whip depression.

Learn to Lean

As the psalmist reflects on God's works, he remembers how God has led His people in the past. When Israel came to the Red Sea in the days of the Exodus, things looked hopeless. The Egyptian army was pursuing hard behind

Banishing Discouragement

them, and an impassable sea was before them. Then, all of a sudden, when it looked as though all hope was gone, God stepped out, the waters backed up in sheer fright, and Israel walked through the sea on dry land. Through wind and rain, thunder and lightning, sunshine and storm, God led them.

Then the psalmist made an astonishing statement. He said that though God had led his people through sea and through storm, "thy footsteps are not known. Thou leddest thy people like a flock by the hand of Moses and Aaron" (vv. 19-20).

Underscore "thy footsteps are not known." The psalmist sang that God led and leads even when we cannot see His footprints. He led through His servants Moses and Aaron.

The truth here is that God's leading is often invisible and imperceptible. His footprints are often unseen, but they are there, nonetheless. He continues to lead His dear children along.

In times of discouragement we must learn to lean on God in faith. We need to believe in His leading, even though we cannot see His footprints in the dust, feel His hand on our shoulder, or hear the whisper of His voice in our ears. May the Lord deliver us from the sensuality of always wanting a feeling. We must learn to pray, "Lord, I don't feel that You are here, but I thank You that You are, anyhow." We often become discouraged because we feel that God is not with us. If we can believe that He is with us even when we cannot feel Him, then it strengthens us.

Perhaps you have read the beautiful anonymous story "Footprints." It goes like this:

One night a man had a dream. He dreamed he was walking along the beach with the Lord. Across the sky flashed scenes of his life. From each scene he noticed two sets of footprints in the sand; one belonging to him, the other to the Lord.

When the last scene of his life flashed before him, he looked back at the footprints in the sand. He noticed that many times along the path of his life there had been only one set of footprints. He also noticed that it happened at the very lowest and saddest times of his life.

This really bothered him and he questioned the Lord about it. "Lord, You said that once I decided to follow You, You would walk with me all the way. But I have noticed that during the most troublesome times in my life, there is only one set of footprints. I don't understand why when I needed You most You would leave me.

The Lord replied, "My precious, precious child, I love you and I would never leave you. During your times of trial and suffering, when you see only one set of footprints, it was then that I carried you!"

Likewise, when we cannot see the footprints of God, we must know He is there carrying us along.

It is as we sometimes sing:

All the way my Saviour leads me;
What have I to ask beside?
Can I doubt His tender mercy,
Who through life has been my guide?
Heav'nly peace, divinest comfort,
Here by faith in Him to dwell!
For I know whate'er befall me,
Jesus doeth all things well;
For I know whate'er befall me,
Jesus doeth all things well.

—*Fanny J. Crosby*

How, then, can we handle discouragement?

First, look in the Book—remember God's works of the past.

Second, keep an attitude of gratitude—praise God no matter what.

Third, learn to lean—trust God when you can't see His working.

The shepherd symbolizes Christ who cares for us, provides for us, and leads us (Ps. 23). He is the Good Shepherd who gave His life for us. We need to affirm our faith in Christ. We need to believe in Him and pray to Him every day. We need to focus on the good that He does for us. This becomes our strength. This is how to handle discouragement.

15
The Days Dwindle Down
(Psalm 90)

In ancient days, before the invention of mechanical timepieces, the Chinese developed a unique way of judging the hour. A small rope was set on fire with knots so arranged that by the time the heavy cord had burned from one knot to another, sixty minutes had elapsed. Every day they would insert a new string of hours in the holder. As they viewed the charred remains of yesterday's rope, they were reminded that "time passed is as ashes" and can never be reclaimed.

Later, people became dissatisfied in marking off time merely in hours, so they invented timepieces to reduce time to smaller and smaller segments. Today we measure time not only in hours but in minutes, seconds, and even fractions of seconds. The result is that we have become slaves to our own devices. Time has remained unchanged throughout the ages, but our relationship to time has changed; today we are almost completely dominated by time. As W. E. Sangster wrote, "We are all slaves to time, and half of mankind is crucified upon a clock."

To our time-conscious age, God speaks a timeless truth. He reminds us to pray: "So teach us to number our days, that we may apply our hearts unto wisdom" (Ps. 90:12).

This verse is a part of a meditation on the brevity and the frailty of life. It is set against the backdrop of the

The Days Dwindle Down

timelessness of God. It begins with the assertion that God has always been. Before the mountains came into being—in fact, before the earth was created—God existed. He has always been and He will always be. He is from evelasting to everlasting (vv. 1-2).

Compared to God, we are weak and frail, and with Him time is nothing. The psalmist wrote, "Thou turnest man to destruction; and sayest, Return, ye children of men" (v. 3). The word *destruction* is best translated "dust." The Bible declares that God made us from dust in the beginning and that we will return unto dust at death (Gen. 3:19; Eccl. 12:7).

A young boy attended Sunday School where for the first time he heard that mankind was made out of the dust of the earth, and that when we die we return to dust. He went home and excitedly told his mother this startling news. She, of course, had known this all of her life and was not awed by it.

She responded, "Yes, yes, now run along and play."

The young lad went into the bedroom to play, and the ball he was playing with rolled under the bed. When he crawled under the bed to retrieve the ball and saw dust everywhere, he scampered out and rushed back into the kitchen, exclaiming, "Mommy! Mommy! Come quick! There's a man under our bed, and I can't tell whether he is coming or going." We did come from dust, as God has told us in Scripture.

To the eternal God, time, which means so much to us, means nothing. A thousand years are to Him as one day or as a watch in the night (v. 4). A "watch" was the amount of time that a sentry spent on duty as he guarded the walls of a city or the camp of his army. The Jews divided a night into three watches. The first was from sunset until ten o'clock. The middle watch was from ten o'clock until two o'clock. The third was from two until sunrise. While a watch in the early morning hours may have seemed like an eternity to a sleepy soldier, it really lasted just a few short hours and was quickly over. To God, a thousand years passes as quickly as a shift of guard duty would pass for us.

Against the backdrop of the eternal nature of God is set the frailty of our lives (vv. 5-9). The writer used four analogies to describe the brevity and frailty of life. He compared our lives to a flood, to a dream, to withered grass, and to a story.

Have you ever seen a person swept away by a flood? I did once. I had just begun my first semester as a student at Baylor University in Waco, Texas, in 1953, when a devastating tornado struck that city. The tornado was followed by torrential rains. I was in the library of the university when the storm came, and I did not fully realize what had happened. When the rains subsided, I left the library and started back to my dormitory. To get there I had to cross Waco Creek which runs through the middle of the Baylor campus. Ordinarily, Waco Creek has only a trickle of water in it. While its banks are ten to twelve feet high, the water is usually so shallow that a child can play in it. But that day, because of the rain, its banks were full of raging, swirling water rushing to the Brazos River. Just as I stepped up on the bridge that crossed the creek, I saw a log with a man clinging to it swept under the bridge and on downstream. Before I could think, act, or even speak, it had come and gone carrying the man away. That's how our life is. It is like a person being swept away by a flood.

Next, our days are compared to a dream. "They are as a sleep" (v. 5). The word *sleep* is best translated "dream." Do you dream much? If you do, then you know that dreams sometimes seem to last all night long—especially if someone is chasing you or you are trying to escape from a "monster." However, scientists who study dreams tell us that dreams actually last only a few seconds. That is the way our life is. It seems so long at times, but it passes as quickly as a dream.

Third, our life is compared to grass that flourishes in the morning, is cut with a scythe in the afternoon, and then withers away by evening. In the hot middle Eastern sun, lush grass cut from its roots soon wilts. So our lives quickly lose the vitality of youth, and we grow old and die.

Finally, our life is compared to a story. The psalmist wrote, "We spend our years as a tale that is told" (v. 9). I wonder if this verse furnished the inspiration for Shakespeare's line, "Life's ... a tale told by an idiot, full of sound and fury, signifying nothing." The point of the psalmist is that stories have a beginning and a moral to them, but then they come quickly to an end.

All four of these analogies depict life as fleeting, passing, and frail. God is eternal, but we are temporal.

The psalmist then declared that ordinarily the most we can hope for is to live seventy years. If, by chance, we are extra strong or in especially good health, we may make it into our eighties. But even then, because of sin, our years are filled with toil and with tears. Our strength is sapped by labor and by sorrow, and we soon die (see vv. 10-11).

In the light of these somber truths, the psalmist was then driven to his knees in prayer for wisdom to know how to live life at its best. At this point he prayed, "So teach us to number our days, that we may apply our hearts unto wisdom" (v. 12).

What does it mean to live wisely today? What effects should the facts that God is eternal and we are so frail have on our lives? How should we live in the light of the brevity and uncertainty of life? A careful study of the specific requests which follow this general petition will tell us. To live wisely means we should live every day to its fullest, we should learn to know God better every passing day, and we should give ourselves to a meaningful and worthwhile work.

Make the Most of the Moment

The first mark of wise living is to live every moment to its fullest. The psalmist prayed that we might "rejoice and be glad all our days" (v. 14). The reason why many people find it so hard to be happy is that they see the past as better than it was, the present as worse than it is, and the future as finer than it will be. In so doing, they fail to make the most of the days which they have.

God has been reminding me in recent days about the importance of seizing and squeezing every moment for the most that is in it. I'm sure that some of these convictions come naturally with middle age, but whatever the reason, I am increasingly aware of how quickly time slips away.

It seems as though it was only yesterday that my children were tugging at my sleeve, asking me to play catch with them in the backyard or to carry them somewhere. I was a young and ambitious pastor in those days, and there was much that needed to be done with seemingly little time to do it all. I had sermons to prepare, committee meetings to attend, people to counsel, and visits to make. Often I just did not feel I had time for them. I would put them off, saying, "Later, not today. I don't have time now."

Today they are grown and gone, and I often wish for those days of yesteryear. I found considerable joy with them then, but I also missed far more because I thought I was too busy.

I think if I could live my life over again I'd not be so busy. Along with Robert Hastings I would stop pacing the aisles and counting the miles so much. Instead, I would climb more mountains, eat more ice cream, go barefoot more often, swim more rivers, watch more sunsets, laugh more, and cry less. I have learned that life must be lived as we go along. The final station will come soon enough.

Thornton Wilder reminded us of this in his play, *Our Town*. Emily Gibbs, who died giving birth to her baby, comes back to the earth and watches herself reliving the morning of her twelfth birthday. It is an exciting occasion at the breakfast table with presents, greeting cards, and kisses from her parents, brothers, and sisters. Through it all, the people in the house, her childhood self included, are rushing about scarcely paying attention to one another. Suddenly, from the unseen she begs them to stop and cries out for them just to look at one another.

But the living are too busy, so Emily sadly bids the earth a last farewell. Then, turning to the stage manager she asks through her tears if any human beings ever realize life while they live it—every minute. The philosopher/stage manager answers that they don't, except for the saints and poets.

It is tragic, but we ourselves so often live life without realizing and enjoying it. Thoreau was right. "The mass of men live lives of quiet desperation." In the business of our daily responsibilities, if we aren't careful, we will move so fast and be so preoccupied that we fail to enjoy every day to its fullest.

Filling the Vacuum

Another aspect of wise living is getting to know God better every day. The psalmist's second petition is: "Let thy work appear unto thy servants, and thy glory unto their children. And let the beauty of the Lord our God be upon us" (vv. 16-17). He prays that the work of God, the glory of God, and the beauty of God will be more and more apparent to us with every passing day. Knowing God is essential to a full and meaningful life and to wise living.

Pascal, the French physicist and philosopher who discovered the vacuum, observed, "There is a God-shaped vacuum in the heart of every man which cannot be filled with any created thing but only by God, the Creator, made known through Jesus Christ."

One of the leading psychiatrists in Europe wrote a letter to a friend in these words: "Those psychiatrists who are not superficial have come to the conclusion that the mass neurotic misery of the world could be termed a neurosis of emptiness. Men cut themselves off from the roots of their being, from God, and life turns empty, meaningless and without purpose. When God goes, goals go. When goals go, meaning goes. When meaning goes, values go, and life turns bad on our hands."

H. G. Wells, the famous historian and philosopher, confessed at the age of sixty-one, "I have no peace. All of life is at the end of the tether." And newspapers reported that Ralph Barton, one of the top cartoonists of the nation, left this note pinned to his pillow before taking his own life: "I have had few difficulties, many friends, great success. I have gone from wife to wife and from house to house, visited great countries of the world, but I am fed up with inventing devices to fill up twenty-four hours per day."

We cannot live apart from God. We can exist without Him, and we can mark time without Him, but we cannot really know life apart from knowing Him. So, part of wise living is coming to know God personally through Jesus Christ and to grow day by day in our relationship to Him.

The Measure of Life

The third essential to wise living is giving yourself to a meaningful and worthwhile work. The psalmist's final prayer is, "... establish thou the work of our hands upon us; yea the work of our hands establish thou it" (v. 17b). The word *establish* literally means "to make firm." His prayer is for God to give a lasting, enduring quality to his life. He wants his life to count.

Since life is so short and death is so certain, we might expect the psalmist to have written, "Why do anything at all? Let's just eat, drink, and be merry, for tomorrow we die." But he says exactly the opposite: "Since life is so short and so fleeting, I want to give myself to that which is lasting and permanently satisfying."

There is a desire for permanence within every one of us, and the nearer we come to the end of life, the more we want our lives to count for that which will live beyond us.

A few years ago a commercial artist who was doing some work for me said, "There must be more to life than just making a living. I want my life to count for more than that." My friend had learned that the best things in life aren't things. Life is at its best when it is committed to a lasting and noble cause, one with eternal significance.

The real measure of a man's life is not its duration, but its donation. We need to pray along with martyred missionary Jim Elliott, "I seek not a long life, but a full one, like You, Lord Jesus."

Did you read what the late Paul "Bear" Bryant said the week before he coached his last college game? "Bear" Bryant was the winningest coach in the history of collegiate football. His teams won 323 games in his illustrious career. But the week before the Liberty Bowl he was asked, "What would you do if you had your life to live over?" He replied, "I would try to be a better Christian."

When the final seconds are ticking off the scoreboard of life, being the winningest coach in history is not all that important. Suddenly, knowing God and living for Him become far more significant. As someone has put it, "Only one life/'twill soon be past,/only what's done for Christ will last." So, it is part of wise living to give yourself to God and His service, so you are caught up in on eternal cause.

If I placed two stacks of money before you—one a stack of one-dollar bills and the other a stack of one-thousand-dollar bills—then gave you a sack and told you you could keep all the money you could pick up in thirty seconds, which stack would you begin with? Since you would have only a limited amount of time, you would be foolish if you did not begin at the place where you could gather the most money in the shortest amount of time.

We all have a limited amount of time. Our supply of this precious commodity will soon run out. Wise living demands that we commit ourselves to those things that will give our lives the most lasting effect. In the light of the brevity and frailty of life, let us resolve to live every moment to its fullest; let us come to know God better with every passing day; and let us devote ourselves to a meaningful and worthwhile work.

16
Does the Lord Live Here?
(Psalm 101:2)

Evangelist Akira Hatori has been one of the leading men in shaping Japan's spiritual history for many years. In his testimony, he shared how he first became disillusioned with Buddhism and was eventually converted to Christianity.[1] As the eldest son in a Buddhist family, it was his duty to offer a bowl of rice and a glass of water every morning on the family's Buddhist altar and Shinto shelf. But he said he didn't have any confidence in these religions because they didn't do any good for his family. His parents used to fight with each other day and night. There was no joy, no hope, no peace, and no song in his home.

Evangelist Hatori became so disillusioned that he tried to commit suicide. Life for him was meaningless; he saw no reason to go on living. Because of this he became receptive to the witness of a high-school friend and eventually committed his life to Jesus Christ. When he told his parents of his conversion to Christianity, their first reaction was anger. His father took him by the neck and shoved him down in front of the Buddhist altar and Shinto shelf and tried to force him to worship the idols, but he refused, saying he would do anything for his father except worship idols.

Christian friends started to visit, to pray for, and to minister to Hatori's family. Eventually his stubborn father came to know the Lord. Then his mother, his sister, and even his Communist brother, who is now also an evangelist in Japan, followed. Among Akira's relatives and family today there are more than twenty-five ministers of the Lord, including one missionary to Thailand.

Did you catch Akira's comment about religion in the home? He had lost confidence in Buddhism and Shintoism because they didn't do any good to his family.

Like Akira, we should hold as suspect any religion that does not help our families. A religion that does nothing for your home will do nothing for your soul, either. To know God vitally is to love Him, serve Him, and live for Him in your home, as well as in your church.

David expressed what should be a goal of every believer's life: "I will walk within my house with a perfect heart" (Ps. 101:2). The word *perfect* means "blameless, upright, in innocence, or with integrity."

These words constitute a solemn vow, a high resolve by David about how he intended to live. The occasion for them was his ascendency to the throne of Israel. At this time his heart was filled with deep gratitude and devotion to God for His many blessings, so he made solemn resolutions about both his public and his personal life. He used the phrase "I will" nine times in the eight verses of this psalm as he expressed how he intended to live and to rule Israel.

It is interesting that he included in these vows an intent to walk within his own house uprightly and blamelessly. Here he is binding himself to good behavior, not only in his public but also, his private life. He vowed to live right, not only as the leader of the nation, but also as the head of his family. He promised that he would be a man of integrity, not only in the council room, but also in his living room. He would walk before God, not only in the state house but also in his own house.

It is never enough just to be a Christian when we go public and appear before men. We must also be Christians before our families. The only kind of faith that can help us is the sort that removes its Sunday robes of ceremony and ritual and dons the work clothes of practicality. We all need to vow, along with David, "I will walk within my house with a perfect heart."

There are three facts about this vow we ought to know. Understanding them will help us make our own commitment to the Lord. It is a needful vow, a difficult vow, and a rewarding vow.

It Is a Needful Vow

Marriage and the home are in trouble today. Already 50 percent of our marriages are ending in divorce. We are rapidly coming to the point where a happily married couple is an oddity in our society. A part of the reason for this is that many people think good marriages simply happen. Most of the people who come to me for premarital counseling are far more interested in talking about the wedding than about the marriage. They realize that it requires time, planning, compromise, and coordination to pull off a good wedding, but they seem to think a good marriage happens automatically; that it doesn't call for maturity, patience, adjustment, and communication to make it work.

Another reason marriages break down is because partners don't consider each other's elementary needs—the need for love, acceptance, appreciation, and encouragement. Instead of thinking of one another we become selfish and thoughtless. In short, marriages fail because people fail, and people fail because they try to live without God.

At the heart of most marital problems is selfishness—demanding one's own way and thinking only of one's self. If we would put one another's rights, needs, and wishes above our own, our homes would be vastly different.

I recently saw a plaque on the wall of a friend's kitchen that expresses this truth. It read: "Home is where each lives for the other and all live for God."

To follow the plain admonition of the apostle Paul in Romans 12:10 would be enough to transform most marriages: "Be kindly affectioned one to another with brotherly love; in honour preferring one another."

A fellow minister was giving a week of lectures at a guided-missile base some time ago. After a service, one of the scientists bared his heart, "You see, my chief problem is not scientific. It is spiritual. I've solved the problem of fusion, but I cannot solve the problem of my marriage. My wife is going to divorce me next month. I can control a bomb, but I cannot handle my boy. My chief problem is not with 'atomic' fallout but with 'human' fallout—husband and wife, father and son. God help us."

I recently heard Bob Breunig, the former middle linebacker for the Dallas Cowboys, share his Christian testimony. He said, "If your home is falling apart, check the foundation first." The best hope a home has for survival is to build on faith in and obedience to Jesus Christ, the solid rock (Matt. 7:24-27). What we need is to commit our lives to Him and then begin, as David, to walk in our own home with a perfect heart.

A Difficult Vow

To walk within our own house with a perfect heart is also extremely difficult. It may seem paradoxical, but I believe it is a fact: It is far easier to live for God in public than in our private lives.

Once a woman was taking a confirmation examination. "What is matrimony?" the young priest asked her. She answered, "Matrimony is a state of terrible torment which those who enter into are compelled to undergo for a time to fit them for heaven." The priest responded in astonishment, "Oh, no, that's not the definition of matrimony. That's the definition of purgatory." The elderly bishop interrupted with, "Maybe she knows more about it than we do." Marriage is more difficult and demanding than most people realize—and for some people it is a terrible state of torment.

What makes it so difficult to live for Christ in the home? Maybe it is because home is the one place where we are our real selves. When we go out in public, we usually put on our best clothes, our best manners, and our most pleasant personality. When we are at home, we normally take off the facades, the veneers, the masks of life, and we become ourselves. There we make no pretense. What we are in the home is what we really are—in mood, manners, and disposition.

We are not always what we appear to be to others. There is a little hypocrisy in all of us—and I do mean all. No one really knows what we are like unless he or she has lived in our home for a while.

John Milton's wife was once referred to as a rose. The unhappily married poet heard about the description and responded, "I am no judge of flowers, but it may be so, for I feel the thorns daily." Many people who are charming and delightful in public are often quite difficult to live with in private.

I am not always the easygoing, sweet-spirited, mild-mannered person in my home that my congregation sees me to be. There are times when I am tired, irritable, and plain old cantankerous. If you lived with me, it would call for abundant grace, understanding, and forgiving. I, too, find it easier to walk with an upright heart in God's house than in my own.

When we really work at living for Christ in our home, as well as in church, our marriages are doubly blessed. I almost never encounter an experience of marital failure in a home where Christianity is a viable factor. Most marriage problems arise because of our selfishness, pride, and downright meanness. Having Christ in our lives purges considerable abrasiveness from our personalities and helps us become more loving, considerate, and sensitive mates. That makes for good marriages.

None of us will achieve complete consistency between our public and private lives. However, that should be the goal of every Christian. We should strive to be consistent at all times. If there is too much variance in what we are in public and what we are in the home, then we are phonies. While no one is the same all the time, we should strive to have as much consistency as possible between what the world sees us to be and what our families know us to be. It is difficult to do, but we should earnestly seek to walk with a perfect heart in our homes.

A Rewarding Vow

Finally, to walk in one's home with a perfect heart is a rewarding vow. I do not know of any place where such a little investment can produce such great dividends as living for God in the home. Someone has expressed it, "Money can buy a house. Add love and you get a home. Add God and you get a temple."

For most of us, a good marriage is necessary to living a happy, fulfilled life. There are some people who have the gift of celibacy—of living alone—and still have a fulfilled life. God grants them that ability. However, for most of us, marriage is essential. That is why God gave us marriage in the beginning—to counter the basic loneliness of our lives.

The Book of Genesis speaks of God's creation. Six times in the first chapter of Genesis, God used the word "good" to describe what He had made. He created the light, and it was good. He made plants to grow and to bear fruit, and that was good. He made the sun, the moon, and the stars, and placed them in the heavens, and that was good. He created the fish of the sea, the fowl of the air, and the beasts of the field, and that was good.

The first thing the eye of God named as not good was loneliness. He said of Adam whom He had created, "It is not good for the man to be alone; I will make him a helper suitable for him" (Gen. 2:18, NASB). The Lord then created Eve from Adam's rib and joined them in marriage. Only after God had created a companion, a counterpart for man, did He say of His creation that it was "very good." The difference between the "not good" and the "very good" in Adam's day was the companionship of marriage. It is often the same with us today.

God wants to be within our marriage from the beginning to make it complete. So, the most rewarding thing most people could ever do to enrich their marriages would be to resolve, along with David, to walk in their own house with a perfect heart.

The worst danger is that we may wait too long to make that resolve. In the closing chapters of the Book of Acts the apostle Paul was on a ship sailing for Rome. The ship docked in a small port to take on fresh supplies, and, as the crew was preparing to sail again, Paul, under the leadership of the Lord, warned the captain and the crew not to continue the voyage because dangerous storms lay ahead. But they paid no attention to his warning and sailed anyhow—right into the teeth of a terrible storm.

So fierce was the storm that they did not see the sun, moon, or stars for many days and nights. The timbers of the ship creaked as it rocked and reeled in the winds and waves. The seamen emptied the ship of its cargo and threw the tackling overboard to lighten it, but nothing helped. It seemed that all hope was gone. At that moment the apostle spoke again. The Lord had appeared to him the night before and assured him that, while the ship would be wrecked, all passengers and crew members would be saved if they would follow his instructions. This time they listened to the preacher, but it was only after all other hope was gone.

This is so often the case with us. By the time most people approach me with their marriage problems, all hope is gone. If they had only listened sooner, if they had only come earlier, if they had only acted when the first storm clouds of trouble appeared on the horizon, the marital ship could have been saved. Somehow they thought they could ride out the storm on their own. Don't let that happen to you. When the dark clouds of discord first threaten your home, turn to God and live closer to Him.

The greatest need of this hour is for us to begin walking within our own house with a perfect heart now. We can do that. The key is found in the recurring statement of this psalm, "I will . . . ." We do what we will to do. We are in control of our lives. We can often be what we want to be and do what we want to do. With God's help we can, if we will.

We can commit our lives to Christ, drawing on His strength daily, obeying His commands. We can walk within our house with a perfect heart. This is needful, difficult, and rewarding. Resolve to begin today. Say it now, along with me and David, from the depths of your own heart, "I will walk within my house with a perfect heart."

17
We Are Beneficiaries
(Psalm 103)

Standing like a mountain peak, Psalm 103 assumes its place among the great hymns of the ages. It is a hymn of thankful praise to God for all His grace. It is perfect and unapproachable. You could not alter it except to mar it. It is a work of supreme devotional art by a religious genius and is one of the beautiful and special treasures of the Old Testament.

Within this psalm there is no prayer, no supplication, and no word of complaint. It is all pure praise.

The psalm divides itself into four logical divisions. The first division is an expression of praise to God for personal blessings (vv. 1-5). Praise does not spring up like a root out of dry ground, however. This hymn emanates from our knowledge of and experience with God. It then grows out of one person's deep sense of gratitude to God who has forgiven him of his sins and delivered him from a sickness that threatened his very life. He has gone to the grave and then been brought back to health. Some of you know what that means.

He began, "Bless the Lord, O my soul: and all that is within me, bless his holy name. Bless the Lord, O my soul, and forget not all his benefits."

What are the benefits the psalmist was talking about? They can be seen in the five verbs of the next three verses.

God is the one "Who forgiveth all thine iniquities; who healeth all thy diseases; Who redeemeth thy life from destruction; who crowneth thee with loving kindness and tender mercies; Who satisfieth thy mouth with good things" (vv. 3-5).

Mark well those five verbs—"forgiveth," "healeth," "redeemeth," "crowneth," and "satisfieth." God had done all these for him.

In the second division of the psalm he praised God for His eternal grace. The psalmist's personal experience quickens his historical imagination. In a moment he moved from his own deliverance to that of his people, Israel. Instantly he was back in the day of Moses. He remembered the Exodus, the long journey through the wilderness, the entrance into the Promised Land, and saw the loving hand of God behind it all. The opening and closing verses of this section stress the universality of the Lord's benevolence and rule (vv. 6-19). The psalmist saw what God did through Moses and to Israel as typical of how God treats all people. Both the revelation through Moses and the whole history of Israel were exhibitions of God's grace to the entire world.

Through Moses, God made known His steadfast love to all people. Israel became exhibit "A" of His justice and righteousness to the oppressed of the whole world.

God's dealings with Israel show us that He is slow to anger (v. 8), and quick to forgive (v. 9), punishing us less than we deserve. "He hath not dealt with us after our sin, nor rewarded us according to our iniquities" (v. 10).

The Four Dimensions of God's Love

There follow four illustrations of God's grace. These show us the four dimensions of His love—its height, breadth, depth, and length.

First, the psalmist wrote, "As the heaven is high above the earth, so great is his mercy toward them that fear him" (v. 11). The psalmist had no idea how far the heavens are above the earth. He could only look up into the sky with his naked eyes and know that it was an immeasurable distance. He was aware that the vastness of space could not contain God's mercy.

We know so much more about the vastness of the universe than he did. We have learned that the farthest object we can see in the universe is perhaps ten billion light-years away. Light travels at a speed of 186,000 miles per second. To know how far ten billion light-years is, you would have to multiply 186,000 by sixty seconds in a minute, multiply that by the sixty minutes in an hour, multiply that by the twenty-four hours in a day, multiply that by the 365 days in a year, and then multiply that by ten billion. That's how far away is the farthest object we can see in the universe.

Imagine that the thickness of this page represents the distance from the earth to the sun, ninety-three million miles, or about eight light-minutes. Then the distance to the nearest star, four and one-third light-years, is a seventy-one-foot-high sheaf of paper. And the diameter of our own galaxy, one hundred thousand light-years, is a three-hundred-ten-mile stack, while the edge of the known universe is not reached until the pile of paper is thirty-one million miles high, a third of the way to the sun!

How vast, how immeasurable is the mercy of God!

Second, he wrote, "As far as the east is from the west, so far hath he removed our transgressions from us" (v. 12). While the psalmist did not know how far the heavens are above the earth, neither did he know how far the east was from the west. His world ended at the Straits of Gibraltar. Beyond that point, he believed, was the end of the world.

We Are Beneficiaries

To travel beyond them was to drop off into nothingness. Today we know that the circumference of the earth is 24,101.5 miles. But that does not measure the distance of east from west.

Don't miss the greatness of this promise. God does not promise to remove our sins as far as the north is from the south, but as far as the east is from the west. God has a reason for expressing the promise like that: there is a limit to the northerly and the southerly directions. There is a North Pole and a South Pole. If you travel north far enough, you will eventually reach the North Pole. Once you have reached the North Pole and go beyond it, you are then traveling south. If you keep traveling south, you will eventually reach the South Pole. Once you have reached it and go beyond it, you are then traveling north again. So, there is a limit to how far you can travel to the north or to the south, but there is no limit to the east or the west. You can begin traveling in an easterly direction and never cease traveling east. You can travel in a westerly direction, ad infinitum.

Third, he wrote, "Like as a father pitieth his children, so the Lord pitieth them that fear him" (v. 13). While we may not understand how high the heavens are above the earth, or how far the east is from the west, we do understand a father's love. While we may not understand it perfectly until we see it in Jesus Christ and hear the story or the Prodigal Son, we are introduced to it here. God loves us like a father loves his children.

Fourth, the extent of God's love is even more remarkable in the light of the fact that God knows our frame; He remembers that we are dust. We are like the grass that grows and withers, like the flower of the field that blossoms and fades. In time we are gone, and it is as though we have never been (vv. 14-16).

But His love is not diminished by the fact that our days are numbered. Against human temporality, the psalmist placed the eternity of God. God recognizes that we are frail, but He bestows fatherly love on us in our weakness. We are as dust, grass, and flowers, but the fatherly love of God to His people is shown to generation after generation. It is "from everlasting to everlasting" (v. 17). We come and go, but His love is constant.

His forgiveness and love for such insignificant creatures as men must lead to universal adoration. Think of it: the height of God's love—as high as the heavens are above the earth; the breadth of God's love—as far as the east is from the west; the depth of God's love—like a father pitieth his children; the length of God's love—from everlasting to everlasting.

Is it any wonder then that the poet wrote?

> Thou didst reach forth Thy hand
>   and mine enfold;
> I walked and sank not on the
>   storm-vexed sea,—
> "Twas not so much that I on Thee
>   took hold,
> As Thou, dear Lord, on me.
> I find, I walk, I love, but, O
>   the whole
> Of love is but my answer, Lord,
>   to Thee;
> For Thou wert long before-hand
>   with my soul,
> Always Thou lovedst me.
>
> —Author unknown

The Doxology

Then, in verse 19, we have the third division of this psalm. The psalmist saw the God who had helped him personally, and the One who loves all the oppressed, as the God who reigns over all the universe. God's dominion over everything, His throne firmly fixed above and over all things, makes His personal interest in us and His love and mercy toward us even more remarkable and deserving of praise.

The psalm closed with a universal summons for praise (vv. 20-22). He called on the angels, the ministering servants of God, all the created works of God in all places to join with him in a mighty chorus of praise to God. He included all creatures, all places, all things.

We sometimes sing:

Praise God from whom all blessings flow;
  Praise him, all creatures here below;
  Praise him above, ye heavenly hosts;
  Praise Father, Son, and Holy Ghost.

That's what this psalm is—a great doxology to God.

Forget Not His Benefits

But what are His benefits to you and me? What do we have to praise God for? Here is a picture of the full measure of God's love. He accepts people as they are and loves them with a love that is not measured by what they do, a love that brings all His benefits to us.

What are the benefits? They are complete forgiveness, constant companionship, and certain hope.

The Full Forgiveness of Sins

The first benefit for which we ought to praise God is His complete forgiveness. This whole passage is shot through and through with that amazing truth. The Lord forgives all our iniquities. He has not dealt with us according to our sins, and as far as the east is from the west, so far has He removed our transgressions from us.

These verses show how completely He has dealt with our sins. With the forgiveness of sins comes a deliverance from guilt and a sense of peace that many do not know. If the world could grasp this truth and enter into God's forgiveness, it would do more for the health and healing of human souls than any other thing I know.

Recently, one of the men in our church sent me some sermon notes made by his little daughter several years ago. She must have been seven or eight at the time. The sermon was entitled, "How to Be a Christian." One of the steps she listed was "throw away your sins." She may have picked up that idea from what Corrie ten Boom once said, "Throw your sins in the middle of the sea and put up a sign 'No Fishing.'"

Technically, we cannot throw away our sins, but the Lord can. He promised in Micah 7:19 to cast our "sins into the depths of the sea." The deepest point in the ocean is the Mariana Trench, located in the Pacific Ocean. There the ocean is 36,198 feet deep. That's almost seven miles. It is equivalent to twenty-seven Empire State Buildings stacked on top of one another. The highest point on the earth is Mount Everest in Nepal. It is 29,028 feet high. That means the deepest point of the ocean goes farther into the heart of the earth than the highest mountain reaches into the sky. That's an inkling of how far the Lord casts our sins from us when He forgives them.

When you begin to think of praising the Lord, don't forget this benefit—the complete forgiveness of sin.

Someone to Hold Your Hand

Recently I called Marietta Crowder's mother to express my sympathy at the loss of her son. Years ago her husband had died. Just a few weeks before, her sister had died. Three days earlier she had buried a son in Dallas. Now another son was dying with cancer in North Carolina. I said to her, "You've really had a hard time lately, haven't you?"

I was trying to comfort her in her sorrow. Instead she preached to the preacher. She said, "Yes, but we have such a great Companion with us to hold our hand, don't we?"

A Companion to hold our hand—we all need that. As Sam Shoemaker put it, "Everybody has a problem, is a problem, or lives with a problem." In the problems of life, we need a great Companion to hold our hand. That's one of the benefits from our Lord.

David had that Companion when he walked through the valley of the shadow of death. The three Hebrew children sensed the presence of that Companion holding their hand when they were cast into the fiery furnace. The apostle Paul wrote concerning his first appearance before the tribunal of Caesar that nobody "stood with me, all men forsook me". Then he added, "Notwithstanding the Lord stood with me and strengthened me . . . and I was delivered out of the mouth of the lion" (2 Tim. 4:16-17). Jesus spoke of that Companion when He said, "And I will pray the Father, and he shall give you another Comforter, that he may abide with you for ever" (John 14:16).

God is committed to watching over us; but He is not over-protective, because He does not want to smother our spiritual growth. He does not save us from these experiences, but He comes to be by our side in them.

Paul speaks of the Lord as "the Father of mercies, and the God of all comfort" (2 Cor. 1:3; see 7:6). The Greek word for comfort is *parakleno*. It means "to call alongside of." It describes the Companion we all need.

We have no idea what will happen to us in the future, but one thing we know won't happen: we won't ever have to walk alone. We will always have a great Companion to walk with us and to hold our hand. That is one of the benefits of our Lord.

Pie in the Sky

The third benefit that comes to all of us is a certain hope of heaven when we die. But I can hear someone say, "Don't talk to me about pie in the sky, by and by. I'm interested in a chicken in the kitchen tonight. I want ham where I am today." That's a part of the "instantism" that is so prevalent in our world today.

We had better be interested in the life to come. Whatever path we take in life ultimately leads to the grave. Whether a man dies in the community where he was born or whether he sets foot on the moon makes little difference as far as the end is concerned. The grave awaits all of us. Medical science may prolong our life and even improve the quality of our life, but ultimately the doctor always fails—every patient will die.

The psalmist reminds us that God knows our weakness and frailty. "He remembereth that we are dust" (v. 14). It would help if we remembered that, also. It would save us from expecting perfection of ourselves. It would deliver us from driving ourselves unmercifully, as though we were superhuman. It would save us from anchoring ourselves too much to this world.

We are as dust. Our days are as the grass. We are like flowers, daisies of the field. The wind whispers over it, and it is there no longer.

When we know the Lord and share in His benefits, death holds no fear for us. Shortly before his death, I spoke with Dr. Morris Ford, pastor of the First Baptist Church, Longview, Texas. He had lived a long and fruitful life in God's service. He said to me, "Death is the least of my worries. It will be the greatest event of my life."

When I shared his comment with a mutual friend, the friend replied, "Morris is in the hope stage of life. Meeting the Lord is very near and very precious to him."

Anybody who knows the Lord as Savior can face death that same confidence and hope. Do you have these benefits in your life? I hope you do, and I hope you will praise the Lord for them. Throughout these verses, people whom the Lord blesses are "those who fear him"? (vv. 11, 13, 17, RSV). The word *fear* means to reverence and respect. As we reverence and respect the Lord and come to Him through the Savior, we experience His benefits and have reason to praise His name.

18
Right Now
(Psalm 118)

There are three time zones in which we may live our lives: the past, the future, or the now.

Those who choose to live in the past are usually either enamored by what they remember as "the good old days," or they are weighted down by guilt, bitterness, and regrets over past wrongs.

The past is a poor place to live. Playwright and novelist Thornton Wilder, who spent much of his life studying past cultures, didn't believe a man should spend much time in his own personal past. "I erase as I go along," he once commented. "I look forward so much that I have only an imperfect memory of the past." Good advice. We should never let yesterday take up too much of today. The past should be a guidepost, not a hitching post.

Other people choose to live in the future. They live their lives on an expectancy basis, always looking for something "out there," completely losing the only value they have—that which is in the present moment. A boy in high school anticipates college; in college, he anticipates the joy that will be his when he lands an engineering job. When he has his engineering job, he believes joy will come when he marries Mary and has a home, and so he goes on anticipating.

I lived much of my life on an expectancy basis, until one

day I realized that the present I was in at the moment was the tomorrow I had looked forward to yesterday. That's when I started living in the now.

We ought to learn from the past; we ought to look to the future, but we ought to live in the now. That was the conviction of the psalmist when he wrote, "This is the day which the Lord hath made; we will rejoice and be glad in it" (Ps. 118:24).

This verse contains both a recognition and a resolution. The recognition is that God made today. Since God made it, it is a good day because He doesn't make anything bad.

There is also a resolution here. "We will rejoice and be glad in it." Most of our days are what we "will" them to be. Occasionally the circumstances of life so overwhelm us that we become their victims. But generally speaking, our days are what we make them.

The resolve of the psalmist should be ours. We should make the most of every day, living in the now.

Making every day a good day does not come just by wishing, but by acting. What can we do to make the most of today? What will help us live in the now? Here are five things that will help.

The Best Part of the Day

First, determine, "Today I will walk with God." The psalmist once said, "In the morning will I direct my prayer unto thee" (Ps. 5:3). Obviously, he had made a practice of meeting God at the beginning of every day and walking with Him. You can't get too far away from the Lord if you start every day with Him.

The importance of the early morning hours in determining the rest of the day cannot be overestimated. Dr. Michael E. DeBakey, the famous heart surgeon, was quoted in a newspaper interview:

For me, the solitude of early morning is the most precious time of the day. There is a quiet serenity that disappears a few hours later with the hustle and bustle of the multitudes.

The early morning hours symbolize for me a rebirth; the anxieties, frustrations, and woes of the preceding day seem to be washed away during the night. God has granted me another day of life, another chance to do something worthwhile for humanity.

Because the early-morning hours are so important in determining the rest of the day, we need to begin them with God.

> The morning is the gate of day,
> But ere you enter there
> See that you guard it well,
> The sentinel of prayer.
>
> So shall God's grace your steps attend,
> But nothing else pass through
> Save what can give the countersign;
> The Father's will for you.
>
> When you have reached the end of day
> Where night and sleep await,
> See there the sentinel again
> To bar the evening's gate.
>
> So shall no fear disturb your rest,
> No danger and no care.
> For only peace and pardon pass
> The watchful guard of prayer.
>
> —Author unknown

Don't Forget to Smell the Flowers

Second, determine, "Today I will find joy in little things." Rudyard Kipling prayed, "Teach us to delight in simple things."

The people who live most nobly have learned to cherish the little happinesses when they come along. Life is not all watching a parade, going to a fire, or spending a day at Disneyland. Most of our lives offer little that is dramatic and overwhelming, but every day has its quota of little happinesses. Where then is happiness found? It is found in having a cup of coffee with a friend, enjoying a quiet meal with your mate, taking a brisk walk through the woods, reading a good book, sitting by a warm fire, and in a job well done.

If we are going to find happiness at all, then we must find it in these little things, these simple things of life, for the web of life is woven of threads like them. When we recognize and cherish them as they arise, we build a reservoir of memory against the sterile hours of life.

Life is to be sipped, not gulped. One reason why many people find so little joy in life is that they are biting off such huge chunks of it that they fail to savor the simple things when they encounter them. So, as Walter Hagen said, "Don't hurry, don't worry, and don't forget to smell the flowers." Remember that yesterday is stale, and tomorrow is not baked, but today, God has given to you. Taste it and see how good one day can be.

Get Outside Yourself

Third, determine, "Today I will do something for somebody else." No day is lived at its best if we live it wholly for ourselves. To make the most of today, to live in the now, we need to get outside ourselves and do something for others.

An ancient legend is told of a man who was tired of living. He went to a wise man and asked to be released from life. In answer, the sage put into the man's hands an herb of healing and advised him, "Go and find seven persons to whom you may give this herb of healing, and, after you have helped them, return to me. Then I will give you release from life." So, the man started on his search. One by one he found seven persons to whom he could give the healing medicine. After the last one had been helped, he returned to the wise man and announced, "I no longer want to be released from life. I want to live!" In the healing of others, he himself had been healed.

That is always the case. When we reach out to help others, we find we are actually helping ourselves. The best way to stop feeling sorry for yourself is to start feeling sorry for someone else!

No one finds life worth living; we must *make* it worth living. So today, do something for someone else. Hug a child! Call your parents! Write a note to a friend! Buy your wife a dozen roses. Do something for somebody else, and you will be doing something to make this day better for yourself.

We are, in a deep sense, what our relationships to other human beings make us. Only as we love and help other people do we keep life from growing sour and brittle.

Choose What You Collect Carefully

Fourth, determine, "Today I will bury all my resentments." It is inevitable as we go through life that people will jostle us, step on our toes, and say and do things that hurt us. It may be a mate who rejects us, an employer who fires us, a neighbor who insults us, or a family member who shuns us. These kinds of things happen to all of us.

If you choose, you can allow them to embitter you. Some people allow the wrongs others do to fester and grow inside them by nursing their memory. Collecting resentments is like carrying a bag of stones. The longer you carry them, the heavier they become. In time your knees will buckle under the weight of them, and they will fall on you and crush you.

Don't you dare collect resentments as you go through life. Collect postage stamps, coins, autographs, or bubble-gum cards if you will, but don't collect resentments.

The moment you start hating a person, you become his or her slave. You don't even enjoy your work anymore because he controls your every thought. Your resentments produce too many stress hormones in your body, and you become fatigued after a few hours of work. The work you formerly enjoyed now becomes a drudgery. Even vacation ceases to be a pleasure.

The person you hate hounds you wherever you go. You can't escape his/her tyrannical grasp upon your mind. When you eat a fine steak it might as well be stale bread. Your teeth chew food, but the person you hate will not permit you to enjoy it.

The person you hate may be miles away but more cruel than any slave driver who whips your thoughts into such a frenzy that your innerspring mattress becomes a rack of torture.

The Bible tells us about such a person. Haman, the prince of Persia, had everything anyone could want—power, prestige, and wealth—but he so hated a Jew named Mordecai that he could not enjoy life. The very sight of Mordecai stirred him to a frenzy of anger and resentment.

Once, after recounting to a friend the glory of his riches, the multitude of his children, and the power of his position in the land, he made a statement that revealed the destructive power of bitterness. He complained, "Yet all this availeth me nothing, so long as I see Mordecai the Jew sitting at the king's gate" (Est. 5:13). His hatred robbed him of peace and contentment and prevented him enjoying the blessings he had—and he ended up hanging on the very gallows he had built for Mordecai.

Resentment always glues us to the past. Like nothing else I know, it gives the person we hate mastery over us.

The Bible warns, "Let not the sun go down upon your wrath" (Eph. 5:26). Don't nurse your anger one single day.

Love your enemies. Go to them and make amends for any wrongs. Pray for them. But never hate them. You can choose to love people and forgive people as surely as you can choose to hate them. The choice is always ours. Remember, always simmer down before sundown.

Live One Day at a Time

Finally, determine, "Today I will trust God for tomorrow." Do you know what the greatest enemy is? It is worry about tomorrow. Jesus, realizing this, teaches us not to be filled with anxieties and fears about tomorrow but rather to trust God to meet our needs day by day.

Then He calls our attention to the birds of the air and the flowers of the field as examples of God's providential care for us. Birds do not plow the soil, plant seeds, or reap the harvest. Yet, their every need is met by the graciousness of God. The lilies of the field do not work themselves into exhaustion or worry themselves into nervous breakdowns, yet no designer ever clothed a client with more dazzling beauty than God does the flowers. Now, if God cares for the birds and the flowers, don't you think we can trust Him to care for us?

Needless worry and anxiety are forms of practical atheism. They are expressions of a lack of confidence in God to provide for our needs tomorrow as He has today and as He has in all of the days gone by.

Jesus closes this teaching by saying, "So don't be anxious about tommorrow, God will take care of your tomorrow too. Live one day at a time" (Matt. 6:34, TLB).

There are two days out of every week we must learn never to worry about or be afraid of—just two: one is yesterday; the other is tomorrow. Yesterday has passed and gone forever. Tomorrow has not yet arrived and is as far beyond our control as yesterday. That leaves only today for us to live and struggle through.

Anyone can fight the battles of today. Any woman can carry the burdens of one day; any man can resist the temptations of today. Only when we willfully add the burdens of those two awful eternities, yesterday and tomorrow—such burdens as only the mighty God can sustain—do we break down. It isn't the experiences of today that drive people mad. It is the remorse of what happened yesterday and the fear of what tomorrow might bring.

God constantly has to teach His children this lesson. When the children of Israel were only six weeks out of Egyptian bondage, they began to worry about how they would live in the future. They even talked about going back to Egypt. They preferred the security of slavery to the risk of freedom. God, in an effort to teach them to live by faith, sent manna from heaven on a daily basis. Any manna they gathered beyond their daily needs spoiled by the next day. God was teaching them to trust Him one day at a time. Later He said to Israel, "As thy days, so shall thy strength be" (Deut. 33:25). And Jesus taught us to pray, "Give us this day our daily bread" (Matt. 6:11).

God has not promised bread or strength for tomorrow. Why should He? Since we cannot eat tomorrow's bread until tomorrow, why worry about it in advance? Since we cannot use tomorrow's strength until tomorrow, why have it? Day by day, He has promised to supply what we need. By all means let us plan ahead, but let us live one day at a time, thinking positively, looking with faith and trust to God, and committing ourselves wholly to Him who loves, understands, forgives, accepts, and empowers us.

There are two principles we need to remember about living in the now. The first, as I have already pointed out, is: this is the first day of the rest of your life. No matter how long you live—whether one day, one year, or fifty—this is still true. This is the first day of the rest of your life, and it could be the last.

The second is this: the future comes just one day at a time. If you will live it from that standpoint, you will live life at its best.

19
Making Peace with Others
(Psalm 133)

A Chinese student told that in his seminary every student was required to memorize four psalms. The first was Psalm 23, which begins, "The Lord is my shepherd." They must be able to say from personal experience, "I know the Lord; He is my shepherd."

The second was Psalm 121, "The Lord shall preserve thy going out and thy coming in from this time forth, and even for evermore" (v. 8). They must be willing to go anywhere without fear and in confidence that God would go with them and would bless them.

They were required to learn Psalm 126, "He that goeth forth and weepeth, bearing precious seed, shall doubtless come again with rejoicing, bringing his sheaves with him" (v. 6). A passion for souls, a broken heart over the sinfulness of the world, is necessary to be effective in God's kingdom.

Finally, they were required to learn Psalm 133, which says, "Behold, how good and how pleasant it is for brethren to dwell together in unity" (v. 1). If they were to be effective in God's service, they had to learn to get along with other people.

Many people realize the importance of knowing the Lord personally. They realize the necessity of being willing to go anywhere with full confidence in God. They also understand the need for having a passion for souls, but they do not realize how important *unity* is in meaningful service and worthwhile living. Consequently, some of the most selfish, proud, quarrelsome, and abrasive people I know are involved in church work. They seem neither to care nor to know how to get along with other people.

A Good and Pleasant Thing

The psalmist gave emphasis to the importance of unity when he described it as "how good and how pleasant" (v. 1). Then he used two analogies to illustrate this. He compared unity to precious oil and to life-giving dew.

The oil he referred to is the oil that was poured on the head of Aaron when he was consecrated, anointed as the high priest of Israel. The oil was poured on his head, ran down his face and beard, and dripped onto his clothing and eventually to the ground. That oil was an outward and visible expression of his inner consecration to the Lord.

Unity is to us what that oil was to Aaron. It is an outward and visible expression of our consecration to God. Jesus taught, "By this shall all men know that ye are my disciples, if you have love one to another" (John 13:35).

It is as simple as this: how can we convince the world that we serve a God of love if we do not love one another? There are no soloists in the kingdom of God. Choosing to be a disciple of the Lord Jesus means joining hands with other Christians in doing the will and work of God. As the ointment on Aaron's head symbolized his consecration to God, so our unity symbolizes our consecration to Him. Let us then always be ready to put aside our petty jealousies, our silly differences, and our sinful pride and get on with giving the world a demonstration of Christian unity by loving one another.

The dew referred to was the tiny drops of moisture that

formed on the plants of Mount Hermon in the early hours of the morning. Dew results from condensation that forms when the cool air of the night comes in contact with the warm leaves of plants. Dew is vital to the plant life of the earth. There are some places where dew actually provides more moisture for vegetation than does rain. Dew, is God's way of watering the flowers and the grass every day.

Unity has that effect on us. It is a source of dynamism and refreshment in life, in any organization, and in any relationship.

This psalm teaches us three important aspects of unity. It teaches us the force of unity, the source of unity, and the course of unity.

Beware of an Independent Spirit

First, the psalm wrote of the force of unity. The power of unity is awesome. It gives strength to a team, a club, a business, or a community.

Several years ago the Philadelphia 76ers basketball team had the greatest assortment of individual talent ever assembled on one team. They were the finest players money could buy. Consequently, they were expected to walk away with the NBA championship. They did well until they met the Portland Trailblazers in the play-offs. Portland was clearly the inferior group of players, but they won the NBA championship. The reason? The 76ers did not play as a team.

After the loss, a reporter asked Coach Gene Schue if his team had a morale problem. He replied, "No, my players are too busy not talking to one another to have a morale problem."

The 76ers had immense individual talent, but there was so much jealousy and individualism that they were not really a team. They lacked unity, and they lost.

Molding individuals into a unified team is what coaches are paid to do. Anybody can learn the fundamentals of the game; books are written on that subject. But welding individuals into a unity is an art. Coach Paul "Bear" Bryant, who became the winningest football coach in history, confided shortly before his death, "I'm just a plowhand from Arkansas, but I have learned over the years how to hold a team together—how to lift some men up, how to calm others down until finally they've got one heartbeat together, a team."

That's the key to success in any realm—getting people working together with one heartbeat as a team.

Static on the Prayer Line

Unity is likewise essential to a good marriage. Peter, in his First Letter, urged Christian husbands to be understanding and sensitive to their wives and to treat them with respect, "that your prayers be not hindered" (1 Pet. 3:7). The word *hindered* is the Greek word from which we derive our word *static*. Conflict in marriage creates "static" on the prayer line that prevents the message from going through. Unity is essential for an effective prayer life and a happy marriage.

Unity is also vital to the church. I am a Baptist by denomination. Baptists have long been noted for our independent spirit. Wherever you have *two* Baptists, you have *three* opinions about everything. One wag commented that "the only thing two Baptists can agree on is what a third one ought to give."

Six men were marooned on an island; two were Catholics, two Jews, and two Baptists. The two Catholics joined together and formed Saint Mary's Catholic Church. The two Jews banded together and formed Temple Beth El. But the two Baptists couldn't agree, so they split; one

Making Peace with Others 191

started Harmony Baptist, and the other, Fellowship Baptist.

While independence is a valued and treasured part of our heritage, it can be taken too far. It must not be allowed to destroy our unity. Many Christians have a bitter spirit, a quarrelsome disposition, and a divisive attitude about them. They lack the loving spirit of our Lord, and thus they hinder His work.

God simply will not work effectively in a congregation that is at civil war. So, be quick to put aside your differences and prejudices and put God's work first.

Soldiers together make an army. Trees together make a forest. Shingles together make a roof. Bricks make a wall. Drops of water make a river. Links make a chain. Flowers make a bouquet. And players make a team. A snowflake is not much, but when enough of them cooperate, they can shut down whole cities. Togetherness is the benchmark of any successful organization, team, club, business, or church.

The Orchestration of Life

Second, this psalm speaks of the course of unity. It enables us "to dwell together." What is unity? Perhaps we can best understand it by looking at what unity is not. Unity is not the same as union. Union is outward, but unity is inward. Union is organizational, but unity is spiritual. You can tie two cats together by their tails, hang them over a clothesline, and have union, but you don't have unity! By the way, a missionary in Japan recently told me that Baptists are like cats. Often when you think they are fighting, they are actually multiplying.

Unity is not being unanimous on an issue. It is not necessary for two people to be in total agreement on everything in order to be unified. We do not have to see eye-to-eye in order to walk arm-in-arm. Two people can be brothers without being identical twins. We can disagree without being disagreeable. We should not fear holding different opinions so long as we do not have an unbrotherly attitude. It is possible to disagree on an issue, to hold to our individuality, and still have unity.

Several years ago we were planning to build a recreation building at our church. While we were in the planning stages, one of the men in our church shared with me his opposition to it. He felt that we should give the million dollars it would cost to missions.

I thanked him for sharing his opinion with me, but I told him that I did not agree. I felt that if we built the building we could give far more to missions in the years to come. Then I encouraged him to continue in prayer about his feelings and to share them with others, especially with the whole church when decision time came. As he left he assured me that should the church adopt this building program, he would do his part in supporting it financially.

We did not agree about the project, but we were unified because we both wanted the will of God to be done, and we both agreed that all of us were smarter than either one of us. We would both bow to the decision of a praying church whatever it might be. We were in disagreement over the issue, but we were unified in our desires and our spirit.

When the issue came before our congregation for a vote, he was the only one who stood in opposition to it. To his credit, though, he was one of the first to make a financial pledge to the building, and, when his work moved him from our city, he paid the pledge he had made before he left town.

That is unity without agreement. There are, of course, some issues in life that must not be compromised. If our position is a matter of conviction, something we have prayed about, we may not be able to turn aside from it lightly. However, we must learn to distinguish between principles and preferences. With principles we need to stand like a rock, and with preferences we need to drift like a fog.

What is unity? It is a singleness of purpose and action. It is a commitment to a cause that is greater than our personal opinions or biases. It is putting aside our personal wishes so we may achieve a common goal far more important than what we would prefer.

The best example of unity I know is an orchestra. An orchestra is made up of many people with many different abilities who play a variety of musical instruments. The only way an orchestra can produce harmony is if each individual musician yields to the will of the conductor, and they all play the same musical score. An orchestra musician cannot choose the music he wants to play. He cannot start and stop playing at his own discretion. Harmony results from each musician's yielding to the will of a competent conductor and playing his part correctly at the right time. The surest way to harmony in life is for us to yield to the will of our Heavenly Father, the Conductor of life.

Unity in Christ

Third, this psalm speaks of the source of unity. "Behold, how good and how pleasant it is for brethren to dwell together in unity" (v. 1).

Our unity is based on our common commitment, our relationship to God in Christ. What causes disunity in any area of life—in the church, in the community, in business, at home? It is always rooted in selfishness and in pride.

Discord results from people seeking their own way and their own glory.

The apostle John told us of a man named Diotrephes who was such a leader. John described him as "fond of being first" (3 John 9, author). That attitude is the first step, the surest way to disunity anywhere, anytime.

Diotrephes would not welcome traveling missionaries into his home or support them in their ministry, and he would not allow anyone else in the church to do so, either. The results were the strangulation of missions and strife in the fellowship. Let us all take warning. Anyone who uses the church as an arena to feed his own ego is an obstruction to God's work. Diotrephes even went around using "sharp, cutting" words against those who did not agree with him. Words are most often the vehicle of strife. As Solomon wrote, "Where there is no wood, the fire goeth out: so where there is no talebearer, there strife ceaseth" (Prov. 26:20).

Diotrephes, like so many today, built himself up by cutting others down. Such selfishness and pride are behind most disunity.

What, then, is the solution to disunity, strife, and division? It is to have the mind of Christ. Paul urged the church at Philippi to unite when he wrote, "Let this mind be in you, which was also in Christ Jesus" (Phil. 2:5). The word *mind* does not refer to Jesus' intellectual grasp, but to His disposition, His spirit, His attitude. What is the attitude or disposition of Christ that we should have? It is His humility. Jesus was in heaven, and, as God, He had every right to reign there and to receive the honor due Deity. But He voluntarily gave up His right to heaven and His reputation in heaven and stepped down to earth to become a servant. He gave up the glory of heaven for the gloom of the cross where He died as a common criminal.

Making Peace with Others

He stooped from the heights of heaven to the depths of humiliation for us.

This is the greatest example of humility in all of history. If we will let that disposition be ours, we can live together in unity. If we hold too tightly to our rights, seek our own ambitions, defend our own reputation, then strife is sure to result.

When we have the mind of Christ, gone will be the petty jealousies, the silly differences, the awkward divisiveness which so often plague churches, marriages, and businesses. When we do not have the mind of Christ, we become a headache to others. We would rather argue than agree. We would rather criticize than commend. We would rather gripe than give. The dissolving of differences in families, at work, and in the church is usually a matter of getting our hearts and minds right with God.

I was in ancient Ephesus several years ago, visiting the ruins of that once-great city. As we walked about the agora, our guide pointed to a carving in the stone sidewalk. It was a huge "X" with a circle around it. The "X" is a Greek symbol for Christ. The circle represented unity. The two joined together symbolized unity in Christ.

Wherever Christians went in the ancient world, they found unity in Christ. Though they came from every country, every culture, and every walk of life, in Jesus Christ their differences were dissolved. Christ and His cause were greater than anything that might have divided them. If we are to find unity in our world today, we must find it in Christ.

Like never before, there is a need for the people of God to join hands and hearts together in the great work of God. We must become a mighty army, unified against evil and for righteousness the world over.

It almost goes without saying, though, if we are to

march as a powerful army for the Lord, we must begin by individually enlisting in His service.

Unity is a good and pleasant thing. It helps to make our service effective and our lives worth living.

20
Heavenly Living on Earth
(Psalm 139)

An old Norwegian tale tells of a boy who found an egg in a nest as he was climbing up the rocky cliffs near his home. He took it home and placed it with the eggs under a goose; it hatched out—a freakish creature! Its deformed feet, unwebbed, clawlike, made it stumble at it tried to follow the little geese. Its beak was not flat; it was pointed and twisted. Instead of having lovely cream-colored down, it was an ugly brown color. And, to top it off, it made a terrible squawking sound! It seemed to be a genetic freak—so ugly and disfigured.

Then, one day a giant eagle flew across the barnyard. The eagle swept lower and lower until the strange, awkward little bird on the ground lifted his head and pointed his crooked beak into the sky. The misfit creature, feeling a kinship to the eagle, then stretched his wings and began to hobble across the yard. He flapped his wings harder and harder until the wind picked him up and carried him higher and higher. As he began to soar through the clouds, he discovered an amazing fact: he was born an eagle, but he had been trying to live like a goose.

We are born to soar. Christians are children of God. The tragedy is that too many of us have never discovered our divine heritage, so we are living a barnyard existence instead of soaring above the mountain peaks of life. Until we know who we are and what we are, we are destined to live far below our potential. But once we see our spiritual heritage, then we know that the sky is the limit for us.

Psalm 139 is a meditation upon the omniscience and the omnipresence of God. As the writer acquaints us with God, he points out the unique relationship we have to Him that makes us special. Realizing this can literally lift us to new heights in our living.

There are three tremendous truths about God in this psalm. First, God is omniscient—He knows everything about us: our acts (v. 2), our thoughts (v. 3), and our words (v. 4). There is nothing, absolutely nothing, about us that God does not know. This fact was more than the psalmist could comprehend (v. 6). It literally blew his mind to realize that God has us thumbtacked to the wall. Of all generations we ought best to understand this. We have built a camera that can photograph a golf ball from seventy thousand feet in the sky. We have built a radar that can track the course of a bumblebee's flight from ten miles away. We have built scales and balances that can weigh the ink in a period at the end of a sentence, cut in half. If we can do all that, surely God, who made all this possible, knows all about us.

God is also omnipresent. He is everywhere (vv. 7-12). To escape His presence is utterly impossible. The psalmist asked a two-part question and then answered it himself. He asked, "Whither shall I go from thy spirit? or whither shall I flee from thy presence?" (v. 7). His answer is: "Nowhere." If we go up into the sky, God is there. If we go down into the heart of the earth, God is there. If we go to the farthest part of the ocean, God is also there. We cannot even hide from God in the darkness of the night. We can't escape Him in the heavens, the grave, the sea,

Heavenly Living on Earth

or the darkness. God is all knowing, and He is ever present.

All of this is a prelude to the primary message of this psalm. The key truth is that our God takes a special interest in every person. David declared: "For thou hast possessed my reins: thou hast covered me in my mother's womb" (v. 13). The word *possessed* means "to create," "to form." The Hebrew word translated *reins* literally means "kidneys." It refers to our innermost parts. The ancients thought of the human anatomy differently from us. The kidneys were looked upon as the seat of a person's thoughts, feelings, and actions. That shouldn't seem so unusual to us. We speak of the heart as being the "seat" of these matters. What's the difference?

Have you heard the story of the little boy who was having a difficult time in his elementary-school anatomy class? His teacher pointed out the various parts of the human body again and again, but he could never seem to get them straight. When she pointed to her shoulder he called it a hip. When she pointed to her elbow he called it an ankle. No matter how hard he tried, he just couldn't learn the various parts of the body.

Then one day something clicked, and he began to get all of the parts right. That day, when the teacher asked him to name the parts of the body, he got every one of them correct. She pointed to her shoulder, and he called it a shoulder. She pointed to her elbow, and he called it an elbow. She pointed to her knee, and he called it a knee.

The teacher was elated. In her joy she said, "Johnny, that's wonderful! You have tried and tried to name the parts of the body, and you just couldn't do it. What happened? How did you finally learn the human anatomy?"

Little Johnny pointed to his temple and said, "Kidneys, Teacher, kidneys."

That's what the psalmist was doing here. He identified the kidneys as the seat of our thoughts, emotions, and actions.

The word *covered* means to "weave together," or "to knit." In poetic language the psalmist pictured God as a master craftsman. In the same way that a weaver takes strands of yarn and weaves them together into a beautiful fabric, so God weaves our muscles, sinews, and bones into a human masterpiece. The psalmist summed up this truth by exclaiming that we are "fearfully and wonderfully made" (v. 14).

But he was not through yet. He continued, "My substance was not hid from thee, when I was made in secret, and curiously wrought in the lowest parts of the earth. Thine eyes did see my substance yet being unperfect" (vv. 15-16).

The word *substance* means "embryo." We are not the product of a giant cosmic assembly line. God prescribed and custom-designed every one of us before our birth. He knew us in our prenatal state. When we were hidden from the eyes of everyone else, we were seen and known by God.

The Bible avows that personhood exists from the moment of conception. This passage extols God for His marvelous work in human creation and constitutes the most important periscope in Scripture for one's self-image.

The psalmist further declared that before we were fully developed, when we were yet "unperfect," God wrote down all the details of our physical characteristics and of our life. Even our allotted days were recorded in God's book before we were born (v. 16). This suggests that our physical characteristics are prescribed by God and not by accident of genetics.

The psalmist concluded by saying that we are continually on God's mind. He thinks about us day and night (vv. 17-18). All this describes God's prior knowledge of the psalmist's life, and ours, even from eternity to conception to birth through death.

God, the Master Craftsman, took the muscles, sinews, and bones of our bodies and personally handcrafted us into human masterpieces. He wrote down both our physical characteristics and our allotted days in His book of records long before we were born. He planned our lives from the very beginning, and we are so valuable to Him that He never gets us off His mind. What a marvelous work of creation we are! What a boost to our self-image! What a challenge to the highest kind of living.

We Are Fearfully and Wonderfully Made

The first truth challenging us to noble living in the psalm is the fact that we are fearfully and wonderfully made. We are not stamped out of the dough of the universe by some cosmic cookie cutter. Nor did we come into being as a result of a celestial assembly line. We are each custom designed, unique. Regardless of our physical characteristics, we are "fearfully and wonderfully made."

Consider the human heart. Your heart is a muscle weighing about twelve ounces that pumps the blood throughout your body. There are more than sixty-thousand miles of blood vessels in your body, and the heart recirculates your blood through all of them every twenty minutes. In the average lifetime of seventy-three years, your heart will beat eight-hundred million times.

Every day your heart pumps enough blood to fill a four thousand-gallon tank car. In a lifetime that is enough blood to fill a string of tank cars from New York City to Boston.

As complex as it is, the heart is one of the simpler organs

of the body. Scientists can make an artificial heart, but they have not tried to imitate such an ostensibly remarkable organ as the liver, which performs so many biological functions that a laboratory of considerable size would be required to duplicate them. We are fearfully and wonderfully made.

Think about the human hand. It is the most magnificent piece of engineering in all creation. Nothing compares to it. There are twenty-five different joints in the human hand. It is capable of making fifty-eight separate and distinct motions. With our hands we are able to pick up a pencil and write down our histories. With that same hand we can grip a hammer and build our civilization. Yet, the same hand is so nimble that a skilled surgeon, using only his thumb and his forefinger, can tie a knot inside a tiny matchbox. We are fearfully and wonderfully made.

Think about the brain. It is a jelly-like substance that weighs about twenty-five ounces and fills your skull cavity. It is sometimes compared to a computer, but to compare the human brain to a computer is like comparing a battleship to a dugout canoe. There are ten billion nerve cells in the average human brain. These nerve cells can be thought of as switching centers that determine mental activity. The largest and most complex computer that mankind has ever made has only *one-and-a-half million* switching centers; our brain has *ten billion!* Normally it has the capacity to record over eighty-six-million bits of information each day. Scientists estimate that the brain's memory banks can hold over *100 trillion* bits of information during an average lifetime. We are fearfully and wonderfully made.

Yet, in spite of that, there are still people who don't like themselves. They grew up poor, their parents divorced, they felt unloved, they failed at something important in life, or someone teased them about some physical characteristic, and they grew up feeling inferior, inadequate, and worthless. They think they are too tall, too short, too skinny, too fat, too hairy, or too bald. Their ears are too big, their eyes bug out, or their nose is too crooked. They focus so much on their outward appearance that they forget the wonder and glory of their inner being. The truth of the matter is that about 90 percent of people don't like their appearance. If they could, they would change something about themselves.

If you have been guilty of feeling bad about yourself, your appearance, or your abilities, stop it! Remember that you are fearfully and wonderfully made.

Remember too that the people who have made the greatest advances in our world have done so in spite of limitations and handicaps. Napoleon was five feet two inches tall.

Beethoven was born with a hearing problem. He was almost deaf at twenty-eight and was completely deaf at thirty. What a handicap for a musician! Yet twenty-five years after he was completely deaf, he wrote his *Ninth Symphony*.

Abraham Lincoln was the son of an illegitimate woman. He had an inadequate education, and he never developed the social graces. He was so ugly that when he walked down the street people gawked at him; he was even called "the original gorilla." Yet he became one of our greatest Presidents.

Thomas Edison, inventor of the electric light, microphone, phonograph, medical fluoroscope, nickel-alkali battery, and hundreds of other devices, was almost deaf. Someone once told him, "It must be a great handicap to be deaf." He replied, "Why, no, it helps me to concentrate. Besides, how many things have you heard today that were worth listening to?" He used his liabilities as an asset that enabled him to concentrate on his work much better.

Many of God's most effective servants have also had handicaps. Moses had a speech impediment. Jeremiah had an inferiority complex. The apostle Paul was possibly lacking in physical stature, may have had bad eyesight, and may have suffered from other handicaps.

John Wesley, the founder of methodism, stood only four feet eleven inches tall and weighed 120 pounds. D. L. Moody was so poorly educated that reading his unedited sermons would make an English teacher cringe. And George Whitefield, one of the most eloquent preachers who ever lived, was an asthmatic. He coughed and wheezed his way through sermon after sermon. He was reported to be so eloquent that he could bring tears simply by pronouncing the word *Mesopotamia*. Benjamin Franklin once went to hear him preach. Knowing of Whitefield's eloquence Franklin left all his money at home lest he became so moved by Whitefield's sermon that he might give it all away. After hearing Whitefield preach, Franklin was so stirred that he borrowed money from a friend and gave it all to Whitefield. That's eloquence!

Whitefield once visited friends in Newport, Rhode Island. When the townspeople heard he was there, they gathered outside the house where he was staying and clamored for him to preach to them. He climbed out of bed, dressed, and stood on the porch, a Bible in one hand and a candle in the other, and preached until the candle went out. Then he went upstairs to bed and died that night with an asthma attack.

We all have handicaps. We all have limitations. But still we are fearfully and wonderfully made. Consider your

Heavenly Living on Earth

limitations as a compliment from God. At certain levels of competition, if an athlete is really good, he is given a "handicap." A handicap can be a compliment from God and not a limitation in life.

So, don't go around complaining about your looks or your limitations. Remember that you are fearfully and wonderfully made and that God can use you uniquely in His service.

It's Just Like the Plan

Before your allotted days began, God had already written down your physical characteristics and His master plan for your life. There is a purpose for your being here. The greatest joy in life is to find and to fulfill God's plan for your life.

Don't ever be guilty of thinking your life is meaningless. If it is, it is because you have made it so by your own selfish pursuits. Your life was built for service and for dedication. Through commitment to God's will you find your highest purpose in life.

When the Golden Gate Bridge in San Francisco was under construction, the architect-engineer of the project became ill. It was necessary that he be hospitalized and then bedridden at home throughout the duration of the construction. Almost daily his workmen came to report on the progress of the bridge. Only after it was completed was he was able to see it. When he saw it, he cried, "Thank God, it's just like the plan."

The finest thing that can ever happen to any one of us is to live life just like God planned it for us. That's what Jesus did. Jesus testified: "My meat is to do the will of him that sent me, and to finish his work" (John 5:35). Later, on the cross, Jesus said, "*It* is finished" (John 19:30). He didn't say, "*I* am finished." He said, "It is finished." What did He mean? He meant God's plan for His life. He meant world redemption, for He had come to "give his life a ransom for many" (Matt. 20:28; Mark 10:45).

Thus it was with the apostle Paul. He lived with the conviction and died with the satisfaction that God's will had been completed. He wrote in the waning days of his life, "I have fought a good fight, I have finished my course, I have kept the faith" (2 Tim. 4:7). The race God had mapped out for him had been run to completion. He had finished what God wanted him to do.

God also has a plan for your life. God was showing you a part of that plan when He made you. He gave you certain talents, abilities, and characteristics that suited you for it. If you will discover them and use them, then you will find the purpose for your existence.

Be careful about comparison. There is always a temptation to look at others and compare ourselves unfavorably to them. I love Billy Graham. How he can preach! How I wish I could preach like that! However, the fact that I can't doesn't mean that I am useless in God's service. There are things I can do that Billy Graham cannot. After all, God created both of us. We must guard against the temptation to so focus on our own inabilities that we fail to use our abilities.

Always on His Mind

The final thought of the psalmist was that God is always thinking about us. We are always on His mind. His thoughts of us are like the sands of the sea, more than we can number. We are the object of His affection. We are the focus of His continual thought.

Jesus taught us that God marks the fall and attends the funeral of every sparrow. God has numbered the very hairs of our heads. We have just passed through the "hairiest" era of American history. Long hair and shaggy beards have been the rage, and my two boys were right in style. In fact there was a time when it looked like everything they ate turned to hair.

Do you know that the average man has one hundred thousand hairs on his head? If he has a beard, there is an average of thirty thousand whiskers in it. The hair on your head grows approximately five inches a year. The hair on a person's face grows approximately five-and-one-half inches a year. We lose from twenty-five to one hundred strands of hair every day, and if we are fortunate, new strands replace those we lose.

That may be more about hair than you want to know, but it is not more than God knows. I remind you that God has numbered the very hairs on your head. If God takes time to do that, surely He is interested in you.

A three-year-old girl came home from Sunday School and said, "Mommie, Mommie, I learned a new song in church today."

"What is it?" the mother asked.

The little girl stumbled around and finally said, "Jesus knows me, this I love . . . ."

The mother said, "Honey, I learned that same little song when I was a girl. I learned it a bit different, but I think I like it your way better."

Sing it any way you like—"Jesus loves me! this I know," or, "Jesus knows me, this I love"—it is just as true either way. He both knows us and loves us.

Though we are fearfully and wonderfully made, though God has a plan mapped out for our lives, and though we are continually on His mind, we have one fatal flaw. We have sinned against God. We have transgressed His laws and are thus alienated from Him. David, king of ancient Israel, saw this fountain of sin within as the source of his inferiority, inadequacy, and failures, so he did what all intelligent men should do when they reach the end of their rope. David turned to God. He stopped blaming his enemies and asking God to destroy them; instead, he fell on his knees in utter humility.

He prayed this prayer: "Search me, O God, and know my heart: try me, and know my thoughts; And see if there be any wicked way in me, and lead me in the way everlasting" (vv. 23-24).

David realized that the place he should start in making things right was with himself. His prayer contains a proper sequence: first, he prayed that God might search him (know him); then he prayed that God might cleanse him; and, last, he prayed that God might direct him.

His steps to God were sincere, logical, and well-thought out. To him salvation was not merely a superficial, emotional experience; it was the biggest, most deliberate decision in life. David's transformation, as a result of his prayer, was full and complete. Salvation comes to you and me in the same way.

Here is the secret for living life above the mountain peaks:

> God formed us,
> Sin has deformed us,
> And Christ, alone, can transform us.

Turn to Him, trust Him with your whole heart, and you can reach your full potential.